AFTER COLUMBINE

A Schoolplace Violence Prevention Manual

by Dr. Kelly A. Zinna
Police Psychologist

This book is dedicated to my husband, Michael, without whose undying love, encouragement and foresight this book would not be possible.

I am also eternally grateful to my parents, James and Dorothy, who instilled in me the courage to pursue my dreams.

All of you have helped make me who I am today.

TABLE OF CONTENTS

Preface   **iii**

Introduction   **v**

Chapter 1   **Columbine – Just the Beginning?**   **1**
                      The Columbine High School Massacre   **2**
                      New Factors Introduced at Columbine   **5**

Chapter 2   **The Evolution of Schoolplace Violence**   **11**
                      Fads vs. Trends   **11**
                      Schoolplace Violence Chronology   **13**
                      Parallels to Workplace Violence   **22**
                      Categories of Violence in Schools   **27**
                      The Copycat Phenomenon   **30**

Chapter 3   **Origins and Dynamics of School Violence**   **33**
                      From Victim to Avenger: Pathway
                            to Violence   **37**
                      T-R-A-I-T-S   A Recipe for Disaster   **46**

Chapter 4   **Threats: An Important Warning Sign**   **53**
                      Categories of Threats   **55**

Chapter 5   **Profiling of Schoolplace Violence Perpetrators**   **59**
                      General Indicators of Violence Potential   **60**
                      FBI Cumulative Offender Profile   **66**

Chapter 6   **Prevention and Intervention Strategies**   **69**
                      Striking a Balance Between Naivete
                      And Paranoia   **70**
                      Preparation   **71**
                      Policy Development   **73**
                      Investigation of Threats and
                            Violent Incidents   **78**
                      Emergency Preparedness   **83**

Chapter 7   Advanced Training Strategies   87
             Front-Line Personnel:
             Teachers, Coaches, Counselors
                 and Support Staff   87
             Community Involvement and Training   89
             Training Students   90
             Surviving a Violent Incident   94

Chapter 8   Violence-Induced Trauma   97
             Critical Factors Following
                 a Violent Incident   98
             Media Management   102
             Post-Trauma Responses and
                 The "Normal" Course of Trauma   104

Chapter 9   The Ripple Effects of Columbine   111

Bibliography   113

About the Author   117

Preface

The images of April 20, 1999 are indelibly etched on the nation's conscience. Sounds of gunfire and bombs exploding, children and adolescents running, literally for their lives. Panic-stricken and terror-filled faces of former innocence now lost to unspeakable terror and the primitive instinct of survival. Their faces are captured, frozen in time, by photographers' cameras. This scene did not arise from a war-ravaged country. Rather, this scene is from just another day at school in America, another day at Columbine High.

The events at Columbine High School may have forever changed the nature of educational institutions in this country. Not that Columbine was the first such tragedy. School violence of this type has been occurring with increased frequency over the past decade. However, Columbine was the one event that America watched unfold on their televisions. Like so many other changes in society, from the placement of stop signs to airline security measures, the action is one of *reaction,* but only when the body count gets high enough. At this time, it is safe to say that most schools are looking at improving security and attempting to find ways to stop violence in their schools. After Columbine, every school district in America, and every parent with a child who attends a school were asking the same questions. "Could this happen here?" "What if that had been us?" While some choose to continue to deny that this type of violence is a serious problem, others are taking action to insure that no matter what, this does not happen at their school.

While Columbine was a shock to many, this kind of violence has been around for some time in the adult world. In fact, it appears that adult workplace violence served as the model for this new type of school violence. The predictors, dynamics and perpetrator characteristics are strikingly similar. The hybrid term "Schoolplace Violence" is used to discuss that subtype of school violence that parallels adult workplace violence. The good news is that many programs have been successful in deterring workplace violence. These same types of prevention programs can likewise be used to stop Schoolplace Violence. Many such programs are discussed in detail in this book, and the bibliography section contains other helpful references. This book is an informative, guidance manual designed to empower school officials in their goal of preventing Schoolplace Violence. It outlines the dynamics and characteristics of this unique type of violence, provides information on how to recognize it, and offers prevention and intervention strategies. Unlike many other forms of violence, Schoolplace Violence is very predictable. It follows a specific course of action and this, in turn, offers many opportunities for intervention and determent. The goal of this book is to emphasize the first steps towards prevention: education and training.

INTRODUCTION

This book serves as a resource for teachers, administrators, school resource officers, and concerned parents who wish to develop a response and prevention plan to handle threats and violence in schools. While many resources purport to help prevent and deter aggression and violence in children, the advice usually comes through avenues of improved parenting and mental health services. In contrast, this manual emphasizes steps that offer immediate empowerment in identifying, preventing and defusing potentially lethal situations. Instead of expounding on broad societal, biological and cultural reasons for increased violence among youth, and essentially telling schools they should select their student body from better families, this book offers "in-the-moment" direction and practical suggestions. It can help school official prepare for and respond to Schoolplace Violence incidents. Since each school setting is unique, administrators should consult with a competent professional to address specific situations.

The material provided in this guide is designed for school administrators, teachers, school resource officers, and parents who already recognize the extensive damage school violence causes, and are searching for ways to address this problem before another incident occurs. The book offers step-by step advice to assist in the early identification, intervention, prevention, and containment procedures that can reduce the risk of school violence.

The nature, scope and levels of school violence are broad. Educational institutions are continually challenged to devise ways to prevent and intervene in each type of violence encountered on school grounds. Physical altercations, gang violence, vandalism, and all-out spree shootings represent just a few of the potential sources of violence operating in schools today. This book outlines the different types of violence that school districts are likely to encounter. However its main emphasis is on a specific type of violence, that which parallels the dynamics of adult workplace violence, "***Schoolplace Violence.***" The dynamics of this kind of violence are identifiable and therefore preventable. This book outlines several measures which, when undertaken by school personnel, can help reduce the possibility of this type of tragedy.

CHAPTER ONE

COLUMBINE – JUST THE BEGINNING?

As the Columbine High School incident unfolded on national television, almost everyone had the feeling they were watching a defining moment in American history. The events and images of that day were played out in real time, and then continuously replayed so they became indelibly etched on the nation's psyche. Those images would forever change the image of schools as a safe haven for learning. The focus of America's attention quickly turned from mourning over the victims, to a desperate search for information about the perpetrators. Human nature has a strong desire to try to comprehend how such a thing could happen, and ultimately a need for solutions for prevention. These things can help us regain some sense of control over a world that, can quickly become a scary and unpredictable place. Information, like that contained in this book, can assist in this need to understand and ultimately prevent similar incidents.

As a clinical psychologist, I was on-scene at Columbine High School and at Leawood Elementary School where parents were being reunited with surviving students. The trauma hung so thick in the air it seemed tangible. Tears stained the faces of countless parents seen walking away from the school clutching their sons and daughters. Parents' faces radiated feelings of unspeakable gratitude that their children had escaped. In the days and weeks that followed, I conducted debriefings for many of the law enforcement and crime analyst personnel who were thrust into Columbine. Later, I attended meetings with the Jefferson County Sheriff's Department, the law enforcement agency primarily responsible for the scene. From this intense work, and my background experience in violence prediction in institutional and workplace settings, I derived valuable information on how to identify and successfully intervene in Schoolplace Violence. I had previously been aware of the parallels between Schoolplace and workplace violence, and, in fact, had authored the majority of this book almost a year prior to Columbine. When Columbine was compared with other violent incidents, the dynamics were strikingly consistent. It is readily apparent at this time that Columbine is not only similar to other Schoolplace Violence incidents, it is part of a trend in violence. Columbine was not the beginning, and without intervention Columbine will not be the end.

THE COLUMBINE HIGH SCHOOL MASSACRE

Shortly before 11:00 a.m. on April 20, 1999, two students, Eric Harris, 18, and Dylan Klebold, 17, stormed Columbine High School heavily armed with a semiautomatic rifle, two sawed-off shotguns, and a semi-automatic handgun. It is believed they had previously planted some 67 homemade bombs, including one that weighed more than 50 pounds; capable of destroying an entire quadrant of the school along with its occupants. Harris and Klebold fired randomly at students and teachers, and then hunted down and killed students who were hiding under desks in the library. At one point, they exchanged gunfire with officers in the parking lot outside the school. The total damage inflicted by the assailants totaled 13 dead, 23 physically injured, and countless others psychologically scarred for life.

Witnesses later reported that Harris and Klebold were ruthless in their attack. They talked and joked with each other as they went about their killings, and took time to drink from water bottles they had brought along. They appeared to enjoy themselves, and encouraged each other to find more victims. Their cold-heartedness extended to statements and questions directed at the victims. For example, asking one female if she believed in God. When she said "yes," she was shot dead. Stories of the cruelty of these perpetrators are unequaled thus far.

By Schoolplace Violence standards this incident lasted an eternity, 30 to 45 minutes, and ended with the perpetrators killing themselves. Unfortunately, the drama and horror lasted much longer for the law enforcement officers, rescue crews, parents and survivors. Approximately 500 law enforcement officers responded, including six

SWAT teams and four bomb squads. Attempts to enter the school were hampered by the threat of bombs, the lack of information about the number and location of perpetrators, and their efforts to escort survivors to safety while simultaneously ensuring that no perpetrators were allowed to escape by posing as victims. Once inside the school, law enforcement officers were inundated with sensory stimulation coming from the incessant ringing of the fire alarm and school bells, and the consistent flow of the sprinkler system that was activated by smoke from the detonated bombs. Teachers and students stayed locked in their classrooms, some of them injured and bleeding, waiting for help. One teacher was badly injured by gunshot wounds but managed to stay alive for hours, still shuttling kids to safety. He died in the arms of a SWAT team member.

A few hours after the incident began, a report of 25 dead was issued. This was later revised to the accurate count of 13 dead, 12 students and the one teacher. Twenty-three other students suffered horrible injuries from the bullets, shrapnel and glass, and some required lengthy hospital stays. All surviving victims are physically scarred. Some are impaired for life. And the survivors fortunate enough to escape physical injury, have psychological scars they wear on the inside. During that afternoon, a helicopter reporter announced he could see several students running from the school to the safety of law enforcement. He optimistically broadcasted, "They are safe! Those students have escaped! They are going to be *all right*!" That is likely a matter of perspective.

About the Perpetrators

As the nation's attention turned from the victims to the perpetrators, a jigsaw puzzle of information about these boys began to emerge. There were no surprises here. They were known to play violent video games, and one of the perpetrators even designed some of his own. They frequented grotesque and sexually deviant websites, and listened to music filled with themes of hate and destruction. They had expressed anger with peers who called them names such as, "Dirtbags, faggots, and inbreeds." They were generally loners, but when they socialized it was with a loosely associated group of nonconformists called the "Trench Coat Mafia."

A week before the killings, Klebold and his father went to the University of Arizona where he had planned to study computer science. The Thursday before the killings, the Marines rejected Harris because he was on psychiatric medication. Harris had a personal website that he used as an outlet for his anger and disgruntlement, sending his hatred of the world into the anonymity of cyberspace. He also used the site to detail instructions for building pipe bombs. Harris listed one of his hobbies as, "preparing for the big April 20th." On the site he wrote, "I will rig up explosives all over town. I don't care if I live or die…A pipe bomb is the easiest and deadliest way to kill a group of people…Goodbye to all on April 20, 1999." A diary was found detailing their desire to kill 500 people at Columbine, and then hijack a plane to crash into New York City. The diary spanned the course of a year, and there were maps of the school showing places to hide, and the largest concentration of students at a particular time.

Examination of the perpetrators' backgrounds revealed that both boys had felony convictions for breaking into a van and stealing about $400 worth of electrical equipment in January of 1998. A few months later, Randy Brown, a parent of another Columbine student, contacted the police about Harris' website and his harassment of Brown's son. Police forwarded a "suspicious incident" report to Columbine High School, but no official action was taken. In February of 1999, Harris and Klebold were released from probation, having been commended for their participation in anger management classes. Their probation officer predicted them to lead successful lives. Allegedly, at some point in the year before the massacre, Harris' father found a pipe bomb in his son's room but did not call the police.

If Harris and Klebold wanted to leave an impression on American society, they may have succeeded. Certainly they received attention. This news story was sent around the world, with extensive coverage provided by almost every newspaper and television station for weeks and months afterward. The only major newspaper to abstain from printing the story on the front page was the *Chicago Sun,* whose editors felt that the media hype may contribute to more such incidents. The media coverage was so extensive that Columbine was recently listed as the third largest news story *of the century.* Why was this? What was so different about Columbine? Certainly similar events had happened before. The answer is that Columbine was different from other incidents in many ways, notwithstanding the sheer number of victims. The following is a description of the new factors in Schoolplace Violence that were introduced at Columbine. These factors appear to usher in a new level of dangerousness.

NEW FACTORS INTRODUCED AT COLUMBINE

Killing Teams: Two Perpetrators Instead of One

With the exception of Jonesboro, Schoolplace Violence incidents have all involved just one perpetrator. While other Schoolplace Violence perpetrators may have had peripheral accomplices, only the Jonesboro and Columbine incidents had two individuals actually involved in the shootings. **Killing Teams** are a departure from past incidents, and represent a more lethal picture due to the psychological dynamics of team assailants. In analyzing these Killing Teams, distinct leader and follower identities emerge. One perpetrator usually possesses a strong and domineering personality, and is more entrenched in violent ideology. The interplay between the two individuals serves several purposes in making them more lethal. These factors are as follows:

1. **Erosion of Inhibitions** Two individuals, devising a plan of violence together, serves to erode the natural inhibitions towards violence more quickly. They reinforce each other's fantasies, and eventually arrive at a point where the plan of violence actually seems like a viable alternative.

2. **The Violent Plan is Elaborated and Reinforced** As each party adds new details and input, the idea becomes more real. A cognitive dissonance aspect also sets in where, having devoted so much time and energy to the plan, the chance of backing out is lessened. Any second thoughts are not voiced or, if one party verbalizes doubts the other quickly refutes them. In this manner the plan becomes fortified, and doubts are not tolerated. A course of violence is set in motion and begins to gain momentum.

3. **Social Reinforcement** Two individuals working together reinforce each other's ideas, and they may even compliment the other on their

5

deviousness. They bond over a mutual interest in violence. Additionally, there is the added pressure to "not let the other down" by failing to follow through with the plan. They also reinforce each other's perception of perceived injustices, propagating an "us versus them" mentality. This dynamic is especially powerful when one considers that almost all Schoolplace Violence perpetrators were described as loners. This pairing over violence may represent the strongest or the only social interaction they have. This reinforcement increases the chances that the perpetrators will execute their plan.

Of course with an increased number of perpetrators, the chances of a higher body count are proportionately increased as well. With more guns and more bombs, more victims are possible. Furthermore, with two perpetrators involved in the actual killing spree, opportunities for intervention are hindered. For example, one perpetrator can keep watch for law enforcement or potential resistance, while the other continues to kill. Overpowering *two* armed assailants is inherently more difficult than overpowering one. Another problem with multiple shooters is accurately determining the number of assailants. It is usually clear when there is more than one, but deciding exactly how many, and where they are, can be extremely difficult. The presence of multiple assailants always presents a significant problem for law enforcement, and this is magnified during events of mass chaos.

Guns *and Bombs* Were Used

Columbine was the first incident where bombs were used in addition to guns. While several Schoolplace Violence perpetrators were reported to have made bombs, they did not use them during the actual assault. Bombs clearly increase the chance of a greater number of casualties. They have "maximum killing power" as Harris once bragged. Of course, part of the media fallout with this incident was the advertisement of the Internet as a source of information and instruction on how to make a bomb. This media attention increases the risk that copycat Schoolplace Violence incidents will continue with this lethal addition. The presence of bombs also increases the difficulty level for law enforcement intervention because, in a sense, the police are out-armed. Additionally, the use of bombs represents an absolute disregard for human life and reflects more evil motivations. In summary, a student's interest in guns should not necessarily give rise to suspicion of violence potential, but an interest in bombs is *always* gravely concerning. There are no pro-social uses for bombs.

The Perpetrators Shot Victims Who Were Hiding
Unlike other Schoolplace Violence incidents, Harris and Klebold searched for, and found some of their victims as they hid under desks in the library. In all other Schoolplace Violence incidents, the perpetrators sought out one or two victims, but fired randomly as well. The methodical search and kill strategy evidenced by Harris and Klebold appears to be a reflection of their determination and the calculated nature of their assault. It should be noted that, despite this apparent anomaly among Schoolplace Violence incidents, the advice stands that hiding is a good way to increase one's chances of survival, and this should be encouraged as part of survival training. Many more lives were saved by hiding than were lost. At Columbine, survivors hid in a variety of places including closets and bathrooms, and even in the kitchen's freezer. This proved to be a useful strategy. (See Chapter 7 for more information on Surviving a Violent Incident).

The Incident Involved Several Areas of the School
Harris and Klebold entered the school through the cafeteria, and proceeded down several hallways and up the stairs to the library. Thus victims were strewn throughout the school. At one point, the SWAT team members were contacted with the information that someone in the Science classroom had hung a sheet outside the window bearing the words, "Help me, I'm bleeding to death." Without the aid of accurate blueprints, it was extremely difficult for the rescue teams to know where the science room was, and where it was in reference to them (see Crisis Management Kit at the end of this chapter). Through much of their rampage, the perpetrators had complete control of the situation by virtue of the fact that they were pro-active, and law enforcement is always reactive. Harris and Klebold had studied the floor plan at length, and had marked out critical areas for mass killing, concealment and escape.

7

Law Enforcement was also Targeted

The perpetrators had made several preparations to forestall rescue attempts by law enforcement, and even fired directly at them at one point. The omnipresent threat of bombs was a significant hindrance. Law enforcement did not appear to intimidate the perpetrators. In fact, they attempted to harm or kill the police in several ways. They fired rounds out the windows at officers and booby-trapped bodies, including their own, with explosives. Due to these active assault tactics on police, and the constant movement by the shooters, law enforcement efforts demanded increasingly complex and cautious maneuvers.

Premeditation and Planning was Extensive

The details involved in the planning and execution of the Columbine massacre were far more in-depth than any previous incident. Harris and Klebold spent a full year planning this assault, and thoroughly considered all aspects of their attack. They marked yearbook pictures of their identified targets. They built several dozen bombs and obtained high-powered weapons. They timed the attack to coincide with the congregation of a great number of students in the cafeteria and library. This intense level of premeditation represents an escalation in the drama and intensity, and ultimately the damage inflicted by Schoolplace Violence episodes.

Victims Were Shot Both In and Outside of the School

As Harris and Klebold walked towards the school, they shot several students outside, and then continued their killing spree once inside the school. In other episodes of Schoolplace Violence, perpetrators attacked and murdered their victims exclusively either inside or outside the school building. This broadening of the "killing zone" made rescue attempts more difficult. Law enforcement and medical personnel felt compelled to address the needs of the victims that they encountered outside, knowing there were likely many more victims inside. Rescue and treatment efforts were further hindered by their need to protect themselves from further attack while still within range of the shooters.

There was an Armed Guard on the School Grounds
In the majority of the other Schoolplace Violence incidents, there were no armed security guards or police officers assigned to the school. Columbine had an armed sheriff's deputy stationed on campus, and Harris and Klebold were aware of this. This departure suggests that Schoolplace Violence perpetrators are becoming bolder and more daring, and may even feel pressure to "out-arm" the guard or officer assigned to the school. There is debate over whether schools with armed security are safer. From analysis of the one Schoolplace Violence incident since Columbine, the one near Atlanta, Georgia where there was also an armed guard on the property, this variable does not seem to make a difference to Schoolplace Violence perpetrators, or to the survival rate of potential victims. However, in all fairness, on-site law enforcement does seem to deter other, less lethal types of violence such as fistfights.

Whether Columbine was responsible for establishing new trends in Schoolplace Violence will be determined with the passage of time. The incident outside of Atlanta certainly varied significantly from Columbine in many ways. Nevertheless, the additional considerations introduced by Columbine have expanded recommendations for school systems and potential targets. Those recommendations are as follows:

1. **Develop a Crisis Management Kit** containing building plans, key phone numbers, locations of controls for automatic building functions (e.g., fire alarms, bells and sprinkler systems), a student roster, and other crucial survival information. The kit should be duplicated and kept in several different places in the event that certain sections of the school are too dangerous to enter. A separate kit should also be kept in a safe location away from the school. This kit should be made accessible to law enforcement personnel as well. The usefulness of this kit depends on updating it on a regular basis.

2. **Predetermine Staging Areas** for individuals who escape from the school as well as locations for medical triage. This should be a well-known and easily located site, e.g. the track and field house or a local

business. A secondary location should also be determined in the event the first one is too dangerous or inaccessible.

3. **<u>A Plan for Reuniting</u>** surviving students and their families should be thoroughly detailed and thought out ahead of time. This information should be regularly dispersed to parents and students. In the event of a Schoolplace Violence incident, this plan should be disseminated to the media to aid those who are unaware of, or have forgotten the plan.

CHAPTER TWO

THE EVOLUTION OF SCHOOLPLACE VIOLENCE

Until the past few years, schools were viewed as safe places for children to go to learn about the world, make friends, develop social skills, and have fun. However, the illusion of schools as safe havens of learning and living has been shattered by recent events. Headlines in the late 1990's depicted these years as some of the bloodiest and most violent times for our schools. The school year 1999-2000 is already being dubbed "The Year of Fear" for American schools.

Over the past decade, several children, all 18 years old or younger, murdered classmates, teachers, and other school officials in a series of Schoolplace Violence incidents across the country. The trend also seems to be increasing in frequency and severity. Despite this, studies by the National Education Association indicate that school is still the safest place for children to be. School is safer than the mall, the street or the home. From the Center on Juvenile and Criminal Justice, we know that the chances of a child being killed at school are one in a million. However, these statistics do nothing to calm the fears of students and parents who are concerned that they may be the next statistic. Nor does it mitigate the school system's responsibility to prepare for this type of crisis. The recent Schoolplace Violence episodes have had, and will continue to have, a significant impact on students' sense of safety and thus, their ability to learn.

FADS vs. TRENDS

Many have wondered if Schoolplace Violence is a passing fad exaggerated by the media, or really a trend in our society. Fads are commonplace in American culture. There are fads in clothing, foods, health and exercise regimes, and hairstyles. Fads gain extreme popularity for a short time and then fade quickly. The world of violence also has fads. An example is the Tylenol poisonings in Chicago in 1982. One individual decided to put cyanide in Tylenol capsules, and this ultimately impacted the way over-the-counter medications were packaged forever. Not too long ago, over-the-counter medication and food products were sold in relatively easy-to-open packaging. At most, childproof caps existed. After the Tylenol tampering incidents, and the suggestion of a few copycat crimes that followed, products were protected with seals and plastic wrapping. This type of violence turned out to be short-lived as companies battled back with tamper-proof packaging. People have adapted to the security measures necessary, and barely realize a violent fad changed the norm of our culture.

Despite being fads, singular events of violence have the capacity to change the course of society. The Tylenol poisonings forever changed the course of packaging of not only over-the-counter medications, but also most food and hygiene products. The Oklahoma City Bombing in April of 1995 changed regulations so it is no longer possible to drive up close to a Federal Building. After the assassination of John F. Kennedy, presidents were no longer permitted to ride in open motorcades. Charles Whitman fired shots from on top of a clock tower at the University of Texas in 1966, killing several people. He was single-handedly responsible for the organization of SWAT teams.

In addition to violent fads, violent trends also exist in society. Trends start slowly and are relatively long lasting. While they also change the course of society, this change is implemented in a much slower fashion. When threats and acts of violence are consistent over time, society is forced to adapt to minimize their impact. Soon, the new adjustment becomes second nature, and people do not consider the security measures to be abnormal. Airport security is an example of the impact of a trend in violence. Before the 1970's, safety checks were minimal and passengers simply walked onto airplanes. However, as terrorism, hi-jacking, and bomb threats increased in frequency throughout the early 1970's, the airline industry was forced to take major steps. Today's airport security measures can be quite intrusive. Before this trend in violence, travelers would have thought a security guard rummaging through their bags was a major violation of privacy. Now, airline passengers have become desensitized to this practice, and may even welcome it. If airports discontinued the security measures tomorrow, many people would likely be too afraid to fly. An important observation in this trend is that changes were implemented only after several incidents of hi-jacking. Change is much slower in the case of trends, and occurs only after society agrees that the violence is not going away.

Is Schoolplace Violence a fad or a trend in our society? Initially, the instances were rare and isolated. A 1990 book on juvenile murder, authored by a leading expert in the field, does not even mention this type of violence. Now, Schoolplace Violence incidents appear to occur with increased frequency and intensity and have become almost commonplace. School systems are beginning to recognize and address this threat. In order to determine if Schoolplace Violence is a fad or a trend, it is necessary to examine the pattern of incidents. The following is a delineation of the most notorious Schoolplace Violence incidents in chronological order:

SCHOOLPLACE VIOLENCE CHRONOLOGY

January 18, 1993: Grayson, Kentucky

Gary "Scott" Pennington, age 17, entered his seventh period English class at East Carter High School, fatally shot his teacher in the head, and held the class of 22 students hostage. When a janitor attempted to intervene, he shot the janitor as well. He used his father's .38 caliber pistol. His motive was revenge against the teacher for questioning his increasingly morbid writings. Scott was an honor student, and before the incident had presented a book report on Stephen King's novel, Rage. The book is about a student who shoots his teacher in front of the class. He had also written in a journal, "They don't give out awards for what I have planned." Convicted as an adult of two counts of murder and 22 counts of kidnapping, he was sentenced to life without the possibility of parole for 25 years.

January 23, 1995 Redlands, California

After being reprimanded by his principal for the school's insistence that he wear a uniform, John Sirola, age 13, walked home, and stole a sawed-off shotgun from a family friend. He immediately returned to Sacred Heart High School, shot the principal in the face, then killed himself. There is some question as to whether or not his suicide was accidental as witnesses claimed he tripped while fleeing the scene. The principal survived.

October 12, 1995 Blackville, South Carolina
Sixteen year-old Toby Sincino was suspended for making an obscene hand gesture. The next day, he entered the teachers' workroom with a .32 caliber revolver, fatally shot a math teacher in the face, and then committed suicide. Another math teacher died of a stress-induced heart attack caused by the shooting.

November 15, 1995 Lynnville, Tennesee
At Richland High School, Jamie Rouse, age 17, fatally shot a teacher in the face with a .22 rifle given to him by his father as a birthday present. He then shot and killed a student, and shot another teacher in the head. Investigators suggest that the student accidentally intercepted a bullet meant for another teacher. Rouse had been in a car accident the previous day and was angry about it. He was also having increased academic difficulties. He told an acquaintance about his plans before the shooting. Convicted as an adult of two counts of first degree murder and one count of attempted murder, he was sentenced to life in prison without parole.

February 2, 1996: Moses Lake, Washington
Fourteen year-old honors student Barry Loukaitis of Frontier Junior High School, arrived at school dressed in black and carrying a deer rifle he took from home. He shot and killed two students and a teacher in an algebra class. He was armed with the rifle, two handguns and 70 rounds of ammunition. A physical education teacher heard the shots and ran into the classroom and confronted the student. Loukaitis covered the barrel of his rifle with a plastic bag and instructed the teacher to put the barrel in his mouth. The teacher grasped the barrel as if he were going to do it, but instead grabbed the gun and pinned Loukaitis to the wall. Loukaitis, a straight-A student, was called a "nerd" by his classmates. He had reportedly been relentlessly teased by one of the students he killed. He claimed he was upset by the taunts of classmates and over the

impending divorce of his parents. He was also reported to suffer from "severe depression."

Before the killings, Loukaitis told a friend he thought it would be "pretty cool" to go on a shooting spree as he had seen in the movie "Natural Born Killers." He was also fascinated with Stephen King's book, Rage. For a class assignment, he wrote a poem about killing with the "ruthlessness of a machine" just weeks before the incident. Loukaitis' mother claimed that he was "real fidgety and uncomfortable" while watching the Pearl Jam video "Jeremy" before the killings. The music video portrays the story of a teen outcast who takes out his angst by shooting his classmates.

In an odd twist, Loukaitis' mother later told the court that she had disclosed her own violent fantasy to her son. She told him that she wanted to kidnap her estranged husband and his lover at gunpoint, tie them up, and force them to witness her suicide. Loukaitis told his mother to write about her thoughts and feelings instead of picking up a gun.

Loukaitis was convicted of three counts of aggravated first-degree murder, one count of attempted murder and second-degree assault, and 16 counts of kidnapping in 1997. He was sentenced to two life terms and 205 years in prison without possibility of parole.

February 19, 1997: Bethel, Alaska
After making multiple threats, Evan Ramsey, a 16-year-old student at Bethel Regional High School, chased fellow students through the halls of the school before opening fire with his shotgun. One student and the principal were killed, and two other students were wounded. The student who was killed reportedly called Ramsey names. After the killings, Ramsey put the gun under his chin and said, "They're not going to take me alive." He surrendered after a short standoff with the police.

Unlike most of the Schoolplace Violence perpetrators, Ramsey's life was full of chaos and abuse. His father, Don Ramsey, developed a reputation as the "Rambo of Alaska," due to his own violent behavior. In 1986, the *Anchorage Times* recieved a political letter written by Don Ramsey, and deemed it unsuitable for publication. He retaliated by arriving at the newspaper headquarters "armed and ready to go to war." He had an assault rifle, with approximately 180 rounds of ammunition and a snub barrel .44 magnum with 30 rounds of ammunition. He was eventually captured and sent to prison. He was released in 1997, just two weeks before his son committed the shooting at Bethel High School.

Evan Ramsey was seven years old when his father was incarcerated. Subsequently, his mother became an alcoholic, and Ramsey and his siblings were remanded to the state's care and lived in a series of foster homes. At one of the homes, he was sexually and emotionally abused. By age 10, Ramsey was contemplating suicide. During high school, his grades were poor and friends noted signs of depression. On the day of the killing, he was angry with the principal for taking away his walkie-talkie. He was tired of people calling him names. Before the incident, he told two friends of his intention to bring a gun to school. One of them taught Ramsey to load and fire a .12 gauge shotgun. Before Ramsey arrived on school premises, a group of students gathered in the second floor library, overlooking the lobby because they were told that "something big was going to happen." Ramsey's two friends were later tried as juveniles, convicted and sentenced, and are eligible for release on their 19th birthdays. Sentenced to 200 years in prison, Ramsey will be eligible for parole when he is 75 years old.

October 1, 1997: Pearl, Mississippi

Sixteen-year-old Luke Woodham is currently serving multiple life sentences for stabbing his mother to death, and then shooting nine students at Pearl High School where he was a student. Two of the students died, including his ex-girlfriend. Seven students were wounded. Woodham called himself a "satanic assassin," and worshipped Adolf Hitler. Witnesses described him as "cool and calm" during the assault. Six other students, allegedly involved in a satanic cult with Woodham, were charged with conspiracy to commit murder. He stated that he felt unloved by his mother (his father had left the family five years before) and rejected by most kids at school. A triggering event appeared to be his mother's refusal to drive him to a friend's house on the morning of the killing. Before the incident, he tortured and killed his dog. He beat her with a club, stuffed her in a garbage bag, set her on fire, and threw her into a pond. Woodham was tried as an adult and convicted in June of 1998. He is currently serving three life sentences.

December 1, 1997: West Paducah, Kentucky

Michael Carneal, age 14, opened fire on a prayer group at Heath High School. He shot and killed three students and wounded five others with a .22 caliber semi-automatic pistol. He was offended at having been labeled gay in the school newspaper and had been romantically rejected by one of the female victims. Carneal was well armed with two rifles, and two shotguns stolen from his neighbor's garage. Raised in an upper middle class family, Michael was a B student. He had warned friends to stay away from the prayer group stating, "Something big was going to happen." Before the shooting, he often referred to a scene in the movie "The Basketball Diaries," in which a student opens fire on a classroom. He frequently played the violent video games "Doom" and "Quake." He had been depressed and as he was wrestled to the ground following the incident, he cried out, "Kill me now!" Carneal was sentenced to life in prison, without the possibility of parole for 25 years.

December 15, 1997   Stamps, Arkansas

Joseph "Colt" Todd, 14 years old, sought vengeance on peers who had picked on him. He hid in a wooded area near school grounds, and shot and wounded two students as they entered Stamps High School. "Colt" told police that he was not specifically targeting the students he shot.

March 24, 1998: Jonesboro, Arkansas

Mitchell Johnson, 13, and Andrew "Drew" Golden, 11, fatally shot four students and a teacher and wounded 10 others. All the victims were female. Johnson and Golden set off a fire alarm to draw their schoolmates outside and they concealed themselves in a wooded area adjacent to Westside Middle School. As the students and teachers exited the building, the boys gunned them down. Mitchell considered one of the wounded students an ex-girlfriend. Police apprehended the boys running through the woods near the school and found them armed with 10 weapons and more than 100 rounds of ammunition. The boys had stolen four handguns and three rifles from Drew's grandfather, and three additional guns from Drew's father. They had packed sleeping bags and a radio in their stolen van. They also brought along a stuffed animal and two bags of potato chips.

Both Johnson and Golden were average students. Before the killing, Johnson had expressed suicidal thoughts, and had told others that he had "a lot of killing to do." He also pulled a knife on a student, and mentioned to a friend, "Tomorrow you find out if you live or die." Johnson played the violent video game, "Mortal Kombat" and listened to violence-themed rap music. The boys were found guilty of murder and were committed to a state detention center. However, due to a controversial juvenile sentencing law, they will be eligible for release on their 21st birthdays.

April 24, 1998: Edinboro, Pennsylvania
During an 8th grade graduation dance at Parker Middle School, Andrew Wurst, 14, shot and killed a teacher, and wounded two students and another teacher. He used his father's .25 caliber handgun. Before the event, he told others about his homicidal and suicidal desires. He had shown a friend a gun he kept in a dresser.

May 21, 1998: Springfield, Oregon
A student of Thurston High School, Kipland "Kip" Kinkel, age 15, murdered his parents in their home in the early morning hours of May 21st. He then watched the comedy cartoon "South Park" on television. A little before 8:00 a.m., he drove to the high school and opened fire on his classmates in the cafeteria. Two students were fatally shot and 23 others wounded. Kinkel used a .22 caliber semi-automatic rifle and two handguns that were gifts from his father. He wore a trench coat during the rampage. Witnesses said, "His face was casual, like it was something he did every day."

Kinkel's motivation appeared to be one of revenge. He was angry with his peers for teasing him, with his parents for confiscating his guns, and with the school for suspending him. On the previous day, he was suspeneded for bringing a gun to school, and was also arrested for possession of a stolen firearm. Friends reported Kinkel was embarrassed about these incidents, and was concerned about being sent to a troubled youth program. Interestingly, he also expressed concern over the shame his suspension would bring to his parents, both well-liked teachers.

Kinkel's middle school yearbook named him "Most Likely to Start World War III." His topic for a class speech was how to build a pipe bomb. His diary contained his "plans to kill everybody," and tales of torturing animals and setting off explosives. Kinkel allegedly boasted to friends about killing his cat and blowing up a cow. He was known to favor violence-themed music by Marilyn Manson and Nirvana. In his Spanish class, he had said, "I wonder what would happen if I shot someone." He told another friend that he wanted to put a bomb under the bleachers at a pep rally and block the doorway so students could not get out. About a week before the murders, Kinkel's parents had grounded him for the summer for defacing neighborhood houses with toilet paper. The police had once questioned Kinkel for throwing rocks at cars from a freeway overpass. After the killings, the police found five bombs, a hand grenade and a howitzer shell casing in Kinkel's home. The homemade bombs were described as "very sophisticated."

April 20, 1999 Littleton, Colorado

Two Columbine High School students, Eric Harris, 18, and Dylan Klebold, 17, stormed the school heavily armed with a semiautomatic rifle, two sawed-off shotguns, and a semi-automatic handgun. It is believed they had previously planted some 67 homemade bombs, including one that weighed more than 50 pounds. They fired at students within their line of sight, and also purposefully searched out students who were hiding. They talked to each other and their victims as they continued on their rampage. Before killing themselves, they murdered 12 students and a teacher, and wounded 23 others. The boys were known to play violent video games, such as "Doom" and "Quake" and Harris had even designed his own violent video games. They visited grotesque and sexually deviant websites, and listened to music filled with themes of hate and destruction. They were described as loners but were above average students. After a break-up with a former girlfriend, Harris staged his own fake-suicide to torment her. They allegedly made a video of themselves role-playing a shooting spree on classmates. When assigned an essay to describe being an inanimate object, Harris wrote about being a bullet. He had previously been prescribed the anti-depressant medication, luvox, to help control obsessional thoughts. The perpetrators committed suicide in the school library.

May 20, 1999 Conyers, Georgia

Thomas "T.J." Solomon, Jr. entered Heritage High School with a .22 rifle strapped to his leg and a .357 magnum inside his book bag. He had obtained the guns from his father's gun cabinet. Despite being a practiced shot, he fired about a dozen rounds from the rifle aiming low. He injured six students and then took the revolver from his book bag and placed the barrel in his mouth. He was talked out of killing himself by the assistant principal. His first words were, "Oh my God, I'm so scared."

Solomon was reportedly despondent over a recent break-up with his girlfriend. His grades had been falling and he was previously on anti-depressant medication. Evidence found in his bedroom showed precontemplation in the form of printouts of bomb recipes, and notes on where to place explosives at the school. The day before the shooting he became embroiled in a bitter argument with two classmates. He ended it by saying he would "blow up this classroom." Later that day, he told a friend he had nothing to live for. His friend told him he was "crazy." Solomon listened to violent lyrics and played the violent video game "Mortal Kombat." Friends described him as quiet, "unless you were talking about guns." Solomon had received a handgun as a present from his parents, but they later took it away when they discovered he was carrying it around with him.

Despite the fact that media attention has expanded the impact of these events, this chronology appears to support the assertion that Schoolplace Violence is a trend in our society. Other evidence comes from the fact that this form of violence is changing school culture. Schools are implementing metal detectors, identification badges and dress codes. They are hiring more mental health professionals and campus security officers. Most schools are developing emergency plans to deal with a crisis situation. The following is a description of some of the violence prevention tactics adopted by various schools around the country.

Examples of Violence Prevention Strategies

- **Redlands, California:** After the shooting death of a principal at Sacred Heart School, the Redlands' community developed several programs aimed at preventing teenage violence. Their "Building a

Generation" program surveyed teenagers to find out what was lacking in their lives and attempted to provide what they needed. A peer counseling and mediation program addresses issues of conflict resolution. A software company called Environmental Systems Research Institute now provides the means to identify those parts of town that are seeing an escalation in teen-related problems.

- **Edinboro, Pennsylvania:** In the aftermath of the murder of a middle-school teacher, this school implemented a community coalition to fund anger management classes. They also revised their curriculum and student conduct handbook to help prevent future violence problems. To increase security efforts, the school staff now wears identification badges, and all school doors, aside from the main entrance, are locked during the day.

- **Jonesboro, Arkansas:** Some districts have hired local police to patrol their campus, while other schools have hired new social workers to provide conflict resolution training for teachers. Lawmakers in Arkansas are debating legislature to make it more difficult for minors to obtain guns.

- **Springfield, Oregon:** Pending concerns about confidentiality, the Springfield school district is considering providing school personnel with information about students with past violent behavior and criminal records.

- **Milwaukee, Wisconsin:** Although they did not directly experience a spree killing, J.W. Riley Elementary School developed a "rapid response communication plan" to warn students and staff of a violent incident. Emergency escape strategies are employed when a coded announcement is transmitted over the PA system.

- **Moses Lake, Washington:** After one teacher and two students were killed, Frontier Junior High School took additional security measures and renovated the school building. They widened hallways to decrease concealment and deter loitering. Surveillance cameras monitor all areas in the school. School personnel now wear identification badges and security guards patrol the halls.

- **Littleton, Colorado**: Columbine High School has implemented several changes for this school year in response to the mass killing there. Students and staff are required to wear identification badges, better lighting has been installed, and a reporting center for students' concerns has been designed. For more detailed information on the changes at Columbine, please see Chapter Nine.

PARALLELS TO WORKPLACE VIOLENCE

Each episode of Schoolplace Violence has paralleled the dynamics of adult workplace violence in several ways. In all of these violence incidents, the perpetrators gave indications and warning signs of impending violence. Almost all perpetrators made threats or threatening statements prior to committing violence. In all incidents the perpetrators were males who evidenced interpersonal difficulties, had a history of being "disgruntled," possessed few coping mechanisms, and had a fascination and/or proficiency with weapons. The following chart depicts these similarities:

SHARED CHARACTERISTICS:
WORKPLACE AND SCHOOLPLACE VIOLENCE

Workplace Violence	Schoolplace Violence
Mostly Caucasian men	Exclusively Caucasian adolescent boys
Injustice history, filed grievances	Precipitating event: social rejection, school expulsion, disciplinary action
Unsuccessful personal history	Isolated, rejected from peers, social outcasts
Fascination with military, weaponry	Fascination with violent music/ movies videos/weapons
Antisocial and narcissistic features	Antisocial and narcissistic features

The following section outlines the various workplace violence factors that are mirrored in Schoolplace Violence incidents.

The Presence of Threats and Warning Signs

The presence of verbal threats prior to workplace violence incidents has been clearly documented in both anecdotal form and empirical research. A study of 300 workplace violence murders found that in 99% of the incidents, the perpetrator had previously made a threat of violence. Some type of threat has been present in 100% of Schoolplace Violence incidents. Most of the perpetrators were surprisingly clear about their intentions, and most made more than one kind of threat. Eric Harris and Dylan Klebold expressed threats in both verbal and non-verbal form. Harris' website declared, "Goodbye to all on April 20th...this will be my last day on Earth." Columbine's senior class picture depicts Harris and Klebold pointing their index fingers at the camera with their thumbs straight up in an "air gun" pose. Clothing, hobbies, class projects, and statements made by Harris and Klebold evidenced their obsession with violence for several months before the massacre. Like adult workplace violence, Schoolplace Violence perpetrators demonstrate many signs and even clearly verbalize their intentions prior to becoming violent. These behaviors and warning signs must be immediately addressed and followed by appropriate action. Intervention could include one or all of the following: parent conference, violence and risk assessment, psychiatric evaluation, police involvement, suspension or expulsion (see Chapter 7 for more information).

Observers "did not know that they knew"

Despite numerous warning signs, individuals who have the ability to prevent tragedy often do not. This has been observed in both work and school settings, and is generally due to a lack of information or training on the predictors of violence. Most people do not have a frame of reference for violence because it is statistically rare. They are almost always shocked when it happens at their workplace or in their school. The quotes, "I never thought it would happen to me," or "How could this happen here?" are ubiquitous following a violent incident. Likewise, the statement "He just snapped" is frequently heard. A classmate made this statement about Harris and Klebold after Columbine, even in the face of evidence that they had planned the attack for a year. Logic dictates that a year in planning is not "snapping." However, it can appear this way when warning signs are ignored or misunderstood.

The defense mechanism known as denial is a powerful hindrance in the detection of threats and warning signs. The cold hard truth is that *it can happen at any school at any time* and training students, teachers, support staff and the school community on how to identify warning signs, report threats and evaluate risk is critical to prevention (See Chapter 7 for more information).

The Perpetrators had a Perceived Injustice History

The characteristic of perceived injustice history has long been documented in workplace violence offenders. The headline, "Disgruntled ex-employee opens fire at workplace" depicts this mindset. An individual with perceived injustice often blames others for their troubles, is a habitual complainer, believes people are out to get them, and has difficulty accepting responsibility for their own actions. They see themselves as victims at the mercy of the world. Harris and Klebold viewed themselves as victims of the high school hierarchy with jocks at the top, and loners like themselves at the bottom. Like most Schoolplace Violence perpetrators their self-concept was defined as outsiders and victims of an unfair class system within the school. Eventually, they saw no effective means of coping other than violence. The significance, however, is that *this is their perspective*. The irony and incongruence in their self-depiction as underprivileged victims was evident to those who pointed out that these perpetrators came from upper-middle class families, and one of the assailants drove a BMW to school.

There were Victims of Choice and Victims of Chance

In every workplace and Schoolplace Violence incident, there are identified targets, Victims of Choice, and Victims of Chance. Victims of Choice are those individuals who may become victims because the perpetrator had some precontemplated reason for searching them out. Victims of Chance are those individuals who become victims simply because they are in the wrong place at the wrong time. At Columbine, the Victims of Choice were reportedly the jocks and minority students. There is some discrepancy over whether the student whose affirmative answer to the perpetrator's question, "Do you believe in God?" made her a Victim of Choice. More likely, she was a Victim of Chance whose response to the question had no bearing on whether she lived or died.

There appears to be a trend toward increased numbers of Victims of Chance in both workplace and schoolplace violence incidents. Many students who were injured or lost their lives were not identified targets of Harris and Klebold. Most of the victims at Columbine were killed simply because they were available, or because they attempted to hinder the perpetrators, as is the case with Dave Sanders and Patricia Nielson, teachers who attempted to direct students to safety and obtain police assistance. The escalation of Schoolplace Violence incidents has resulted in a prediction of increased numbers of Victims of Chance. Simply, more bodies translate into more notoriety, which may be a motivating factor for some perpetrators.

While Harris and Klebold reportedly threatened their Victims of Choice with the website statement "All jocks must die!" However, the irony of them looking for jocks in the school library is noteworthy. This provides evidence that their Victims of Choice were loosely defined, and were more likely simply a convenient target for their rage. While there is reason to believe they held racist views, and reportedly subscribed to White Supremacist ideology, very few of their victims actually fell into a target group that would logically follow from that purported ideology.

Running from the Building Was a Good Survival Strategy
The images of Columbine students literally running for their lives has been etched into the memories of all who were glued to their televisions on that fateful day. In fact, this strategy has helped save lives in many other incidents of workplace and Schoolplace Violence, and should be the first rule for survival. At Columbine, many individuals were saved when they found an opportunity to run from the school. An example of a workplace violence incident where this strategy was successful was at the Ottawa, Canada bus terminal shooting in April of 1999. Upon hearing the first shots, an employee pulled the fire alarm and many lives were saved when 300 building workers were quickly evacuated from the building.

The exception to leaving the building, of course, is when the perpetrators are outside, as in the case of Jonesboro and Stamps,

Arkansas. In these cases, staying inside actually increased survival. To increase chances of survival, individuals should make every attempt distance themselves from the perpetrators (See Chapter 7 for more information on Surviving a Violent Incident).

Negotiation was Futile

As with all documented workplace and Schoolplace Violence episodes, the perpetrators were unwilling to negotiate. Negotiation tactics work best with those who are ambivalent about their actions, these perpetrators are not. The primary motive of Schoolplace Violence perpetrators is revenge. Therefore, there is not much a negotiator can offer. For the Schoolplace Violence offenders, violence is the means and the end. Additionally, Schoolplace Violence assailants are often suicidal and feel they have nothing to lose, and nothing for which to bargain.

For some criminal offenders, violence is simply a means to an end. That is, violent acts such as kidnapping and robbery are necessary to obtain the final goal, usually money. Unlike these criminals, Schoolplace Violence perpetrators are not suddenly finding themselves in an unpredicted situation, as is the case with bank robbers who are besieged at the bank by law enforcement. These perpetrators are determined to carry out their mission, which is violence based, and in all incidents to date have been resistant to non-violent options. Usually, Schoolplace Violence incidents happen so quickly that negotiation is not even attempted.

Closing and Locking Doors Diverted the Perpetrators

As with many workplace violence shootings, several Columbine students and teachers escaped harm by closing and locking classroom doors, turning off the lights, and remaining quiet so as to not draw attention to themselves. This strategy is effective because individuals on a shooting spree do not typically take the time to overcome obstacles. Harris and Klebold followed this pattern. As they encountered locked and/or barricaded doors, they attempted to gain entry for a brief time, taunting the people inside, but quickly gave up. Schoolplace Violence perpetrators typically feel pressed to operate at a high rate of speed because they know time is not on their side. Concealment and blockades can therefore be very effective in saving lives.

Playing Dead Worked

If one cannot flee the scene, a good line of defense is to play dead. Many students who were injured in the Columbine library remained motionless, hoping that the attackers would assume they were dead. This strategy can be incredibly difficult, because the sound of the gunfire causes a startle reaction. Playing dead is also difficult due to the impaired ability to control one's breathing in high stress situations. Most often, however, perpetrators do not take time to insure that individuals are dead. They are preoccupied with moving on to other targets or escaping pursuers. In a workplace violence incident in Greeley, Colorado, Robert Helfer raised his gun to shoot at a co-worker and a female worker, Karla Harding, lunged at him. Helfer's bullets hit Harding's hand, shoulder and thigh, and she fell to the floor. Alive and in intense pain, she lay still until he left through the window. Ironically, playing dead may have saved her life.

CATEGORIES OF VIOLENCE IN SCHOOLS

Incidents of Schoolplace Violence are inherently different from the more "traditional" violent acts that have been demonstrated in schools for some time. Every episode of violence has its own unique etiology. Motivations of the perpetrator can range from an internal psychotic state, to perfectly sane individuals who have a history of feeling mistreated and disrespected by the world, and seek revenge and power through violence. This is the dynamic most frequently seen in workplace violence incidents. Since the causes of child and adolescent violence is so varied, successful prevention and intervention hinges on understanding the indicators, and taking appropriate and timely remedial action. As with episodes of workplace violence, indifference to warning signs, lack of education, and ignoring potential problems can seriously escalate the situation. Schools have a legal and ethical duty to minimize this risk. The first step towards this goal is determining if, and when, an institution is at risk. It is the responsibility of all school personnel to identify, address and prevent violence from passing through the schoolhouse door.

Analysis of violence that occurs in schools reveals different types and functions of the aggressive behavior. The dynamics differ depending upon the type of violence perpetrated, the motive, goal, and function of the actions. Incidents of school violence can be categorized according to their dynamics:

Traditional Violence
This is the oldest type of violence in school settings, and probably the most common. This category includes fistfights, pushing, shoving, and hair pulling, all of which have long been perpetrated by students against other students. This type of violence is seldom if ever lethal. Even in those rare cases where a fatality occurs, the perpetrator's intent is not usually murder. This type of violence may be a gateway to the more serious forms of violence that are outlined below.

Vandalism
This type of violence is also long-standing in school history. It includes destroying and/or marring school property and school buses, spray painting, team sport pranks, and incidents of breaking into vending machines and automobiles. While most acts of vandalism are minor, vandalism should be considered as a predictor of Schoolplace Violence when the words or images indicate threats of violence. Through these acts of violence against inanimate objects, perpetrators gain momentum and "practice" what it feels like to inflict violence. Graffiti in the boy's bathroom at Columbine High School predicted, "Columbine will explode one day. Kill all athletes. All jocks must die." In hindsight, this was a powerful predictor.

Psychotic Violence
This type of violence stems from a student's disturbed internal mental state and is caused by mental illness or the ingestion of various substances. With drug use increasing at younger ages, this type of violence is likely to rise. Current statistics report figures from between 1 out of 10, to 1 out of 5 children suffer some emotional or psychiatric disorder. Most of these do not include psychotic features, in which the child is out of touch with reality (e.g., hallucinations or delusions), but the presence of a mental disorder may heighten the child's risk for

violence. The majority of students who have been involved in Schoolplace Violence incidents were not officially diagnosed with a mental disorder before their killing sprees. However, many of these students had histories indicating depressive symptoms, antisocial and narcissistic attitudes, and obsessional thought patterns.

Gang Violence
This type of violence has indelibly marked the environment of many large, inner-city schools. Gang violence manifests itself in student-on-student, and/or student against school personnel. This category of violence usually has a specific target, but victims of chance can be caught in the crossfire. The motivation and offender profile for this type of violence is drastically different from the Schoolplace Violence offender. Motivation for gang violence often revolves around drugs and revenge on rival gang members. Perpetrators are commonly members of racially oppressed groups and live in urban areas. Schoolplace Violence offenders have largely been Caucasian loners from suburbs and rural areas. While Eric Harris and Dylan Klebold were members of the now notorious "Trench Coat Mafia," a group of outcasts some might consider a gang, violent behavior was not the norm for the other members of this group.

Schoolplace Violence
The newest category of violence follows the pattern typically seen with adult workplace violence. The perpetrator has a history of perceived injustice, minimal social support, an unsuccessful personal history, poor impulse control, and the violence is in response to an identifiable triggering event. Unlike other forms of violence occurring in schools today, warning signs always precede this type of violence, thereby making it predictable in its nature and course. Through detailed analysis of these incidents, it is apparent the violence was the culmination of a series of stages, escalating factors, and triggers for the perpetrator. In most cases, no one identified or heeded the warning signs in time to prevent tragedy.

While there is no standard procedure for evaluating a person suspected of being a violence risk, a general rule to follow is, ***the more*** *information the better*. Detailed and copious information allows for increased accuracy in assessing the type of violence, identifying likely targets, and predicting when the violence might occur and how the attack will be manifested. Comprehensive information can be utilized to maximize the safety of potential victims. It is recommended that violence assessments and predictions be made using multiple data sources, with benefit of the maximum amount of information obtainable.

THE COPYCAT PHENOMENON

A violence risk factor specific to youth is that they are extremely susceptible to the influences of social learning. Adolescents seem especially predisposed to mimic behaviors that are highly visible, and this can include innovative methods of murder and destruction. This means the "copycat" phenomenon is especially prevalent among young people, and is a potentially lethal learning tool. As one student mentioned in the aftermath of the Springfield, Oregon massacre, "It's a copycat thing. You watch a cooking show and learn how to cook. You watch the news and learn how to kill." While it is impossible to absolutely confirm a copycat crime, in the absence of a perpetrator's admission of such, extreme similarities and the time proximity to previous incidents can provide evidence for this conclusion. The following examples illustrate this point.

- In January of 1993, Scott Pennington held his class hostage in Grayson, Kentucky. Less than a year and a half later, Clay Shrout held his high school class hostage in Union, Kentucky. Both used their fathers' pistols.
- In 1995, John Sirola, Toby Sicino and Jamie Rouse all shot their teachers or principals in the face.
- On November 15, 1995, Jamie Rouse killed one teacher and one student at Richland High. Shortly after, Jamie's younger brother Jeremy was convicted of solicitation to commit murder when he tried to recruit friends to "finish the job" his brother started. Jeremy stated that he was angry that some students alleged he encouraged

his brother and could have prevented the shootings. Jeremy spent two years in a juvenile facility.

- On December 15, 1997 "Colt" Todd of Stamps, Arkansas shot students from the perimeter of school grounds as they entered school. Fifteen months later two boys in Jonesboro, Arkansas shot their classmates from woods near the school.
- Loukaitis, Kinkel, Harris and Klebold all wore dark trench coats, as did the character in the movie "The Basketball Diaries."
- Carneal and Loukaitis had both read Stephen King's novel, <u>Rage</u>. In the story, a boy takes his class hostage and murders his teacher. King wrote the book under the pseudonym Richard Bachman during his own difficult teen-age years. He told Court TV that he recalled the feeling of "rejection, of being an outsider, what it was like to be teased relentlessly, and to entertain the visions and fantasies of revenge on the people who'd done it to you..."

In the wake of the Columbine shootings, countless schools around the country found themselves grappling with threats of bombs and other Columbine-related threats.

- Three days after Columbine, five junior high school students in Texas were charged with conspiring to kill students and teachers at Danforth Junior High School.
- In Wilkes-Barre, Pennsylvania, classes were canceled after a bomb threat was reported in an Internet chat group.
- In April and May of 1999, as many as 30 youth in the state of Texas were investigated, held for questioning, and/or charged with suspicion of plans for school violence alleging involving bombs. A search of the suspects' homes revealed crude explosive devices, gunpowder, and Internet documents with instructions on bomb making.
- Eight days after Columbine, a 14-year-old former student known by his peers as, "Everybody's punching bag," entered W. R. Myers High School with a sawed-off rifle under a long parka. The student fired shots in the hallway, killing a 17-year-old boy and seriously wounding another.

Suspected copycat violence was also evident in Colorado.

- Two weeks after Columbine, four teens plotted an attack on Adams City High School, just outside of Denver. An informant provided written plans, detailed drawings and a map of the building allegedly assembled by the teens.
- A Kennedy High School student was arrested following his exposed plot to blow up the school. As in the Columbine shootings, he created a "hit list" of students he was planning to kill. A local police officer later stated that the youth told him, "It would be Columbine all over again."
- In May, 1999, a senior high school student near Fort Collins, about 60 miles north of Denver, was banned from the after-prom party because he had threatened to "blow up everyone there."

* A recent Gallop poll reported that 37% of 13 to 17 year-olds nationwide had heard of Columbine-style threats at their schools.

This series of events makes it difficult to discount the notion of copycat dynamics operating among youth. It appears to be a real phenomenon that accounts for an increased number of incidents after a major Schoolplace Violence episode. School administrators need to be aware of this in order to provide effective intervention. This is especially true after a Schoolplace Violence incident that receives high media coverage, or occurs in close proximity to their school.

CHAPTER THREE

ORIGINS AND DYNAMICS OF SCHOOL VIOLENCE

A violent individual, or one who presents an imminent danger, is defined as the **Perpetrator.** The potential recipients of violent actions are **Targets**, while actual recipients of violence are **Victims.** The following section describes the characteristics of these individuals, and provides demographic and background data when available.

PERPETRATORS

Thus far, perpetrators of Schoolplace Violence have exclusively been Caucasian males, aged 11 to 18 years who were students at the school. Since this group has consisted exclusively of males up until this point in time, this book's use of the pronoun "he" when referring to perpetrators is statistically accurate. Analysis of these young males reveals they have several traits in common. They have a history of perceived injustice, are described as loners with poor social adjustment, possess minimal coping skills, and have a fascination with lethal weaponry. From the data available at the time of this writing, all but one had made a threat prior to becoming violent. Regarding that one individual, a prior threat was not documented but is suspected to have occurred. The perpetrators initially have a "victim mentality," and at some point their self-identification is transformed to that of "Avenger." The exact process by which this happens is explained in detail later in this chapter. There appears to be a concentration of these types of incidents in certain geographical areas in the United States. The table on the following page summarizes Schoolplace Violence perpetrator characteristics that have been identified thus far:

Characteristics of Schoolplace Violence Perpetrators			
Demographics	**Characteristics**	**Total # (n=15)**	**Pct.**
Sex	Male	15	100%
Race	Caucasian	15	100%
Age	Preadolescent to Teenage (11-18)	15	100%
Geographic Region	South	8	57%
	Northwest	4	29%
	Southwest	2	14%
	North	1	7%
Population Area	Rural/Suburban	15	100%
Characteristic	**# Yes**	**# No**	
Verbal threats prior to incident?	14	0	93%
Gun from home?	12	1	86%
Precipitant discipline/rejection?	14	0	93%
Interest in military/occult/weaponry?	11	0	73%
Social outcast?	15	0	100%
Teased/felt victimized?	12	0	80%
Suicidal?	9	0	60%
History of severe mental illness/ psychosis	0	15	0
History of extreme violence or police involvement?	2	13	14%
Chronic anger?	11	1	79%
Interests in violence (TV, movies, music, video games)	12	0	80%

Adapted from McGee, J. P. & DeBernardo, C. R. <u>Classroom Avenger Profile.</u> Unpublished manuscript.

VICTIMS

Who were the victims of these violent rampages? They were teachers, principals, janitors, ex-girlfriends, hated peers, and innocent bystanders. The chart below summarizes the characteristics of the victims:

Location	Total Dead	Total Injured	Student Victims	Teacher Principal Staff	Parent Victim	Perp Suic (?)
Grayson, KY	2	0	0	2	0	No
Redlands, CA	1	1	0	1	0	Yes
Blackville, SC	3	0	0	2	0	Yes
Lynnville, TN	2	1	1	2	0	No
Moses Lake, WA	3	1	3	1	0	No
Bethel, AK	2	2	3	1	0	No
Pearl, MS	3	7	9 (1x-gf)	0	1 mo.	No
Paducah, KY	3	5	8	0	0	No
Stamps, AR	0	2	2	0	0	No
Jonesboro, AR	5	10	12(1x-gf)	2	0	No
Edinboro, PA	1	3	2	2	0	No
Springfield, OR	4	23	25	0	2	No
Littleton, CO	15	23	35	3	0	Yes
Conyers, GE	0	6	6	0	0	No

Adapted from McGee, J. P. & DeBernardo, C. R. Classroom Avenger Profile. Unpublished manuscript.

Victims of Choice

A Victim of Choice is the perpetrator's direct target, the one against whom they are seeking revenge. In Schoolplace Violence incidents, victims of choice were identified in a specific or general manner. Victims of Choice are usually chosen out of revenge for past instances of rejection or insult. Eric Harris amassed a "hit list" of approximately 15 students who had teased or taunted him. Ironically, none of his intended targets were reported as injured or killed.

Perpetrators	Victims of Choice
Gary "Scott" Pennington	Teacher
John Sirola	Principal
Toby Sincino	Principal
Evan Ramsey	Principal, student who teased him
Luke Woodham	Mother, former girlfriend, Students who picked on him
Joseph "Colt" Todd	Peers who picked on him
Mitchell Johnson	Ex-girlfriend
Kip Kinkel	Parents, peers who teased him
Eric Harris,	Jocks, Minorities, Those who
Dylan Klebold	believe in God (?)
TJ Solomon	Student who teased him

Victims of Chance

A Victim of Chance is an individual who just happens to be in the vicinity of the violence. With increasing frequency, victims of chance are outnumbering victims of choice. There are several reasons for this. The victim of choice is not readily available, the victim of chance obstructs the perpetrator's target or most simply, the victims of chance are readily available. In many cases, even when the victim of choice is available and acted upon, the perpetrator gains momentum through the violence, and redirects the attack toward the next available person. This pattern was clearly evident with Eric Harris and Dylan Klebold, as they encouraged each other to shoot more people.

Some victims of chance are caught in the crossfire or suffer unintended harm from the perpetrator. In the Blackville, South Carolina case, Toby Sincino intended to kill the principal who had suspended him. Instead, he shot and killed a teacher, and another teacher subsequently died of a heart attack from the stress of the event.

There seems to be a pattern developing in the ratio of Victims of Choice to Victims of Chance. When Schoolplace Violence incidents first surfaced in the mid-1990's, the identified targets were often principals and teachers, while the victims of chance (e.g., students and other staff) were often harmed or killed trying to obstruct the perpetrator. Since then, the victims of choice have expanded to include generalized peer groups. As the scope on victims of choice increases, the potential number of victims of chance increases exponentially. For example, if a perpetrator sought revenge on one classmate, that classmate would be the victim of choice. Potential victims of chance are all the others students in the same vicinity at the time of the shooting. Now consider the possibilities if the perpetrator has four or even forty victims of choice. Because of their proximity, victims of chance are also at risk for stray and deflected bullets, shrapnel from bombs and hostage situations.

FROM VICTIM TO AVENGER: PATHWAY TO VIOLENCE

In each of the Schoolplace Violent incidents, the psychological and behavioral pathways leading to violence are very similar. The perpetrators follow a predictable course, marked by distinct psychological stages, as they move from feeling victimized to being an Avenger. Along the way, there is a series of perceived, and perhaps real, injustices that usually consist of rejection or discipline. A wife walks out, a girlfriend ends a relationship, a boss disciplines, or peers taunt the perpetrator. Initially, the individual feels victimized and this feeling begins to occur with increased frequency. Their outlook becomes tainted, and they begin to view all events through a filter of **perceived injustice**. At some point it becomes too much, and they begin to

37

mentally retaliate through creation of revenge fantasies, which often include violence. Slowly, a plan forms. The fantasies persist but eventually they are not enough and the individual starts to act out; testing the environment and *practicing*. If there is no significant intervention, and a triggering event occurs, the individual becomes an *Avenger*. There are four major stages in the process whereby an individual becomes a perpetrator. They are outlined as follows:

Stage 1: Feeling Victimized

Stage 2: Perceived Injustice

Stage 3: Initiates a Resolution

Stage 4: Becomes an Avenger

A multitude of intervening variables can occur between each of these stages. Elaboration on the dynamics of each stage, with explanation of the intervening variables is described in the next section.

STAGE ONE: FEELING VICTIMIZED

Almost everyone can remember times in their life when they felt taken advantage of, slighted or rejected. These are universal experiences for any person living in a social environment. Certainly, most people would agree that organized schooling is a breeding ground for this type of behavior. As the old saying goes, "kids can be cruel." They tease peers for any number of reasons – being too fat, too skinny, too tall, too short, having red hair or a funny name, being klutzy, wearing the "wrong kind" of clothes...the list goes on. Most individuals escape these experiences with few emotional scars. However, for those individuals who are more sensitive, or have terrible home lives, or simply too little resiliency, these experiences can leave deep scars and may eventually breed intense anger. This is especially true during the adolescent years when one's self-concept is poorly defined and the impact of being ostracized or teased can be devastating. Many of these experiences, along with other factors can determine how an individual deals with this type of experience. These factors are known are "intervening variables."

Intervening variables in Stage One:

<u>Temperament</u>
Anyone with more than one child knows that children are born into the world with their own individual personality and temperament. Some kids are just born tough, while others are more sensitive. Those with more fragile constitutions may be unable to emotionally defend themselves against these insults. In turn, anger and resentment may start to build.

<u>Life Context</u>
What is the individual's overall life like? Do they have unusual stressors? The majority of Schoolplace Violence offenders came from "fatherless" homes. Some had an overachieving sibling. Those individuals with an impoverished life context, lacking any particular talents or skills, with dysfunctional family systems, may be at risk to advance on the pathway to violence.

<u>Role-Modeling</u>
Role-modeling is a factor that can powerfully influence a child's direction in life. Children often learn from their parents how to handle stress, anger and rejection. The imprint of these experiences can distinctly affect a child's "blueprint" for coping with the harshness of the world.

STAGE TWO: PERCEIVED INJUSTICE

The individual who has felt victimized for a very long time may eventually adopt a mindset of "Perceived Injustice." This becomes the filter through which all of their experiences are interpreted. This filter distorts minor slights into major acts of aggression. No behavior toward them is accidental. They believe everyone is out to get them. They begin to voice their dissatisfaction, complain of unfair treatment, accuse people of lying to them, and trying to deceive them. Their trust in humanity is significantly decreased and they go on the offensive.

Intervening Variables for Stage Two:

<u>Exposure to Violence</u>
The research on whether viewing violence causes people to become violent is still quite mixed. However, viewing violent material does have a profound impact on those individuals with a predisposition toward violence: it makes them more violent. Watching violent movies, listening to violence-filled lyrics in music, playing violent video games was a common factor found in almost all, if not all, of the Schoolplace Violence perpetrators. Do these actions *cause* violence? Probably not. But it has been clearly shown that exposure to violence, in whatever form, has a desensitizing effect on perpetrators. After continued exposure to violent movies, the individuals no longer feel the repulsion or disgust they may have initially felt. There is a wearing down of one's innate distaste for bloody and gory scenes.

The fantasies of the Schoolplace Violence offenders were most likely reinforced by their music. Harris and Klebold favored a German band known as the Rammstein Boyz, whose lyrics were filled with violent themes. A sample of this group's lyrics are: "You in the schoolyard/I'm ready to kill and nobody here knows of my loneliness...We announce Doomsday/There will be no mercy/Run, run for your lives...You believe killing might be hard/But where are all the dead coming from."

Desensitization and the next step, brutalization, are side effects from exposure to violence that contribute to the development of an individual's violent tendencies. Eric Harris frequently visited websites on the Internet that showed graphic pictures of real human death and dismemberment. These pictures are accompanied by glorifying captions about the subject matter. Sexual brutality further objectified the bodies in many pictures. Clearly, desensitization from these forms of visual violence can increase one's mental ability to carry out destruction and violence. The following list was abbreviated from an anonymous personal website titled "Things I learned from video games."

- There is no problem that cannot be overcome by violence
- If it moves, KILL IT!
- One lone "good guy" can defeat an indeterminate number of "bad guys." "Bad guys" move in predictable patterns. Except for "bosses," most "bad guys" can be dispatched with one hit. You often fare better against a large mob of "bad guys" than against a "boss" in one on one combat
- You can smash things and get away with it. Smashing things doesn't hurt.
- In driving, you can knock other vehicles off the road and get away with it
- If someone dies, they disappear
- If you get mad enough, you can fight even better than normal
- The operation of a weapon is a simple and obvious procedure
- You never run out of ammunition, just grenades
- Death is reversible (but only for you!)
- Although the enemy always has more aircraft than you, they fly in elaborate patterns which make it easier for you to shoot them all down
- Shoot everything. If it blows up or dies, it was evil
- Carpe diem! You only live three times!
- 200 to 1 odds against you is NOT a problem

Lack of a Positive Peer Group

Most Schoolplace Violence perpetrators were described as loners, or kids on the fringes of society. When they did socialize, it was frequently with other adolescents who subscribed to extremist hate ideologies. Racism, Devil worship and identifying with figures notorious for their violent acts (e.g. Hitler) were almost always common threads. The lack of a positive peer group means these individuals are not afforded the opportunity to learn pro-social ways of coping, and to develop healthy outlets for their negative feelings. Most importantly, they are cheated out of good reality testing for their thoughts and ideas.

Availability of Negative Role Models

With the sensationalization of each new Schoolplace and workplace violent incident, there is a proliferation of negative role models being held out for view and potential idolization. History certainly has its share of bad guys as well. Even potentially positive role models, like sports figures, often receive attention for their violent antics. Basketball superstars Dennis Rodman and Latrell Spreewell recently garnered significant media attention for their misbehavior. Rodman was accused of kicking a cameraman who got in his way, and Spreewell allegedly choked his coach during an argument. While millions watched in horror, Mike Tyson committed one of his many highly publicized acts of gratuitous violence, by biting the ear off his boxing opponent, Evander Holyfield. Ex-Dallas Cowboys Head Coach, Barry Switzer, attempted to carry a handgun onto an airplane. And the sports figures who engage in domestic violence? Well, they are simply too numerous to mention here. From these incidents, young people are sent several messages. Violence is an acceptable means of dealing with your problems. It is okay to disregard the law when it suits you. The real damage, however, is perpetuated by society's response to these incidents. In too many cases, and especially when a sports figure or famous person is involved, the message is one of excessive tolerance. Unfortunately, excessive tolerance breeds negative role-modeling.

The Role of the Media
There is much debate over whether media coverage of violent events causes others to become violent. Some people claim that it "gives people ideas." This is probably true in a "copycat" sense, where the individual feels he can do it bigger or better. The FBI profile of Schoolplace Violence offenders lists one of its criteria as "seeking notoriety; attempting to 'copycat' other school shooting incidents but attempting to do it 'better' than the last offender." But the real damage is that media coverage is another form of exposure to violence. This can cause the individual to become desensitized, and can make violence an acceptable alternative.

The research has repeatedly demonstrated that violence increases after a major violent incident, regardless of the type or perpetrators. The number of assaults and murders has been documented to increase after highly publicized events of aggression, like a state execution or a major prize fight. Observations regarding the chronology of major workplace violence incidents also support this finding. On April 19, 1995, the Murrah Building in Oklahoma City was bombed. Not to be upstaged, the Unabomber, Ted Kazinski, put one of his package bombs in the mail the very next day. On April 21, 1995, there was a workplace violence incident in a grocery store in the Denver area where Albert Petroski killed his estranged wife, a deli manager and a sheriff's deputy responding to the 911 call. During his police interrogation, Petroski made reference to the Oklahoma City bombing, pointing out that 163 people had been killed in that incident whereas he had only killed three. These incidents appear to provide supporting evidence for the notion that "Violence begets Violence." Therefore, it seems logical that media coverage of Schoolplace Violence incidents does promote further incidents.

Anonymous Venting
The wide-spread use of the Internet has resulted in computers becoming a kind of "electronic therapist" for the angry and disgruntled. Individuals can now disclose their deepest, darkest, most detailed fantasies of revenge to a glowing computer screen. These are then sent out into Cyberspace without repercussions, or reality testing from the faceless recipients. This sort of venting serves several purposes for the perpetrator. They are able to step into a world where they are powerful and in control, where no one can hurt them, and where they can wreak havoc if they so choose. This activity serves to reinforce their fantasies as they experience instant relief and, more importantly, begin to feel empowered. This point is illustrated by Eric Harris' use of internet monikers. Initially, he choose the name "Rebldomakr" (Rebel Doom Maker). By the end he was "Reb Domine" or Lord of the Rebels.

Unfortunately, this activity also fosters social isolation, a particularly negative side effect for young people who may already be dangerously lacking in social skills. This Anonymous Venting activity is usually conducted alone, in the privacy of their bedrooms with only the computer hardware to witness the frightening transformation.

STAGE THREE: INITIATES A RESOLUTION

With the correct mixture and dosage of intervening variables, the individual begins to blur the line between fantasy and reality. They are no longer satisfied sending their hate into Cyberspace or finding mental relief with fantasies, and a real plan begins to take root. Still feeling powerless most of the time, they begin to concoct elaborate fantasies of revenge. In these fantasies, they develop the details of the victims, witnesses, times, places, and the actual dynamics of the violent act. This fantasy world becomes a primary coping mechanism, and their ability to problem-solve is increasingly narrowed. The satisfaction they receive from these thoughts only goes so far, however, as the Schoolplace Violence perpetrators begin to act on their revenge fantasies. Threats, vandalism, and cruelty to animals are common before an attack on their intended targets. The desire to act upon their fantasy becomes a mission. Eric Harris wrote on his website, "…We plan out and execute missions. Anyone pisses us off, we do a little deed to their house. We have many enemies in our school, therefore, we make many missions…I will rig up explosives all over a town and detonate each one of them at will after I mow down a whole f---ing area full of you snotty a—rich mother f—ing high strung godlike attitude having worthless piece of s— whores…I don't care if I live or die in the shootout. All I want to do is kill and injure as many of you p--- as I can…."

Intervening Variables in Stage Three:

Practicing
This is a very distinct and noticeable element in this stage, and the response received can determine the outcome. During this stage, the individual begins to dramatize their thoughts. They may engage in animal torture or killing, destruction of property or milder forms of violence. In doing this, they are building up enough nerve to actually go through with their plan. This practicing can take many forms. In the case at Columbine, Harris and Klebold collaborated on a video depicting them attacking a house with toy guns and shooting real guns at trees. They wrote extensively about rocket launchers, grenades, shotguns, bullets, and death in their class papers. Other blatant examples of this include taking a toy gun, or an unloaded gun to school. It is only one small step away from the real thing.

In many ways today's society promotes this practicing in a thinly disguised manner. A video game exists called "Postal" that offers players a script for a workplace or Schoolplace Violence massacre. In this game, a disgruntled, raincoat-clad man shoots down police, churchgoers, pedestrians, and other innocent bystanders while muttering, "Going postal." The game especially rewards the killing of law enforcement targets by moving the player to a higher level after achieving this goal. In the end, the "postal dude" must commit suicide to win the game.

This "practicing" stage is perhaps the most crucial because individuals are testing the environment and pushing limits. If they are met with resistance, and ideally some sort of positive intervention, they can still be diverted. If not, they are likely to gain power through their manipulation and intimidation of others. This power is very intoxicating to someone who has felt powerless for a very long time. Of course, as with other addictive substances, the more they get, the more they want. It is absolutely necessary to intervene when practicing behaviors are noted, and to intervene before the momentum is too great.

Threats or Threatening Behavior
The emergence of this factor suggests that the individual is willing to verbalize their intentions. Threats are a powerful indication that violent behavior is not far behind (see chapter Four). Threatening behaviors include non-verbal gestures or significant changes in the individual's countenance or demeanor, or obsession with weaponry and violence (e.g. experimentation with bombs).

Problem-Solving Narrows
The individual becomes less aware of other coping mechanisms, and increasingly fixated on violence as a very real solution. They are playing out violent revenge fantasies on a regular basis now. They may lose interest in other activities and appear depressed. Their obsession with violence pervades every aspect of their lives. With diminishing alternatives, they are rapidly approaching a point of no return. The only ingredient missing now is a significant triggering event.

STAGE FOUR: BECOMES AN AVENGER

There are no intervening variables in this stage. The perpetrator has decided that violence is not only an acceptable alternative, it is the only one. They have changed their self-identity to that of an Avenger. This transformation is extremely empowering. The perpetrator feels confident and in control, perhaps for the first time. It should be noted that there are almost an infinite number of actions that can be taken to prevent Schoolplace Violence, until the perpetrator draws first blood. Once that happens, the chance of de-escalation is dramatically decreased, and tragedy is almost inevitable.

T-R-A-I-T-S

A RECIPE FOR DISASTER

In order for Schoolplace Violence to occur, several factors must be present. The assailant must believe he can gain access to the target or targets, and complete the act before apprehension. There must be either an external catalyst, or an internal emotional reaction that triggers the decision to act. The formula to assess the possibility of violence is identified by the acronym **T-R-A-I-T-S.** This acronym stands for:

TIME
RESOURCES
ABILITY
INTEREST
TRIGGERING EVENT
STUMBLING BLOCKS

Each of these factors can be evaluated and/or measured as part of a violence risk assessment. Many of the factors can be controlled. The individual components of this acronym are explained as follows.

Time
This refers to the period of time necessary for the perpetrator to devise and complete an act of violence. The individual must have ample time to formulate and design a plan, overcome any inhibitions to engaging in violence, gain access to the intended victim or victims, and execute the act. Eric Harris and Dylan Klebold spent almost a year planning their assault on Columbine High School. Rather than risk being deterred by chance factors inherent in an impulsive spree, they planned their assault

to coincide with times when large groups of students would be congregating in the cafeteria and library. Because they entered the building unimpeded, Harris and Klebold had time to move freely about the school and execute their plan. School administrators can remove the time factor from the equation by acting quickly in response to threats and other concerning behaviors. They can also design intervention plans when they believe a threat is imminent.

In those instances where the perpetrator is known, the student's access to school property must be controlled. This is usually accomplished by posting a photograph of the suspect at entryways and, in cases of severe threat, hiring outside security and/or using the community resource police officer.

Resources
This factor refers to the individual's access to guns, weapons, weapon-making plans and materials, as well their mental resources for devising a plan for violence. At this point in time, it appears that "financial resources" are rarely a determining factor in the commission of Schoolplace Violence acts. Analysis of previous incidents reveals that most of the weapons used came from the homes of the perpetrator and/or his relatives, or were obtained from friends. Additionally, the low cost of many firearms, and the ease with which crude bomb-making materials can be obtained, makes the economic resources of the perpetrators virtually irrelevant.

The individuals' mental resources can be measured in terms of intelligence, persistence, organization, and creativity. The majority of Schoolplace Violence perpetrators possessed average to above average intelligence. A student's intelligence can be inferred from teacher reports and academic records. The histories of Schoolplace Violence offenders reveal several honors students in the group. In the Columbine High School case, both Harris and Klebold were above-average students whose combination of intellect, creativity, and violent motives became a reoccurring theme in their high school activities. Harris designed his own website, which he used to detail his hate-filled messages and violent fantasies. Before the massacre, they utilized their intelligence to create explosive devices and to meticulously plan their attack. The student's level of organization is also important here. A perpetrator may have a great deal of intellectual ability, yet be so disorganized they are unable to adequately plan and carry out a violent act.

Ability

The level of threat is directly proportional to the perpetrator's ability to commit a violent act. Ability specifically entails the requisite physical expertise to carry through with a violent plan of action. When assessing a potential perpetrator's ability, one must consider the individual's past experience with and knowledge of weapons, as well as their organizational skills and hand-eye coordination.

A significant factor in evaluating ability is the individual's proficiency with weapons. The individual who threatens to shoot someone must have the gun knowledge and skill necessary to pull the trigger. Almost all the Schoolplace Violence Perpetrators had previous experience with guns. A significant warning sign, even in isolation from others, is knowledge of and experimentation with explosives. Kip Kinkel, Eric Harris and Dylan Klebold became experts in assembling pipe bombs and other explosive devises. As previously mentioned, there are no pro-social uses for bombs, therefore this is always cause for grave concern.

Another aspect of ability refers to capability. Is the individual *capable* of committing violence. Several factors contribute to this assessment but an important one is desensitization to violence. A good illustration of how this works comes from the military. Previously, the military would train soldiers for shooting proficiency with shapeless targets. However, they found that when in an actual combat situation, and faced with another human being, the soldiers were reluctant to shoot. So the military designed targets that were more true to human form, even adding facial features and hair. When soldiers were trained using these targets, they were not nearly as likely to hesitate when faced with an actual combat situation. This demonstrates that a wearing down of natural inhibitions to kill is necessary for people to commit violence.

There appears to be a parallel between these training modes and the intense "training" that today's youth receive from violent video games. These games offer the same skills: hand-eye coordination, desensitization to violence, visualization, self-control, and mental rehearsal of violence. Harris and Klebold demonstrated how this phenomenon could be transferred from fantasy to reality. Harris mastered the video game Doom and its even more violent sequel, Doom 2. In this game, he created floor plans designed as new levels of the game that reportedly resembled his neighborhood and Columbine High School. The scenes he created climaxed with mass killing during which the player could switch into "God mode" to become invincible.

To assess the factor of ability in a potential Schoolplace Violence perpetrator, one should look at the student's extra-curricular activities. Do they include things such as paintball, violent video games with human forms, and viewing violent movies? All these experiences serve to desensitize the individual to violence and make actual violence more of a real possibility.

Interest

The potential perpetrator's interest in violence can be measured through their words and behaviors. This variable exists on a continuum from absolute zero, extreme distaste for violence, to intense fascination and obsession. Almost all Schoolplace Violence perpetrators had a strong interest in guns and other means of destruction. For those who had prior experience with guns, the interest usually extended beyond the occasional hunting experience with friends and relatives. It became an obsession. Gun proficiency in homes where hunting and target shooting are common practices is not usually cause for concern. When someone becomes totally consumed with weapons, and is very animated and enthusiastic when speaking about them, the violence potential has increased.

A good illustration of this is the Schoolplace Violence perpetrator in Georgia, T.J. Solomon. He was depicted as undergoing a dramatic transformation when talking about guns. He would become very animated and excited when talking about or viewing his father's gun collection, but was rather quiet and withdrawn the rest of the time.

Interest in inflicting injury or death must be present at a serious level in order for violence to occur. When it has reached a significant level, it is referred to as obsession. The interest has built to the point that the individual experiences it as overwhelming, a deep-seated drive or compulsion. Without significant intervention at this stage, the individual will likely escalate to the point of violence.

Triggering Event

Before Schoolplace Violence occurs, there is always an identifiable event in the perpetrator's life that results in their making the final decision to engage in violence. The triggering event is usually something external to the perpetrator; the break-up of a relationship, a disciplinary action or suspension, or a parental divorce. However, it can be internal as well. The compulsion to kill may escalate, or depression may overwhelm them and the need for relief becomes unbearable. The triggering event always precipitates the violence and if known, can offer an opportunity for preparation and intervention. A triggering event frequently seen in the early Schoolplace Violence incidents was the break-up of a romantic relationship. This makes sense when the following factors are examined: an adolescent who has limited capacity to handle his emotions, no positive social outlets, absence of role models and overexposure to violence. Couple these factors with overwhelming feelings of rejection and abandonment, and the break-up becomes a classic triggering event for violence.

Another common triggering event is encountering trouble with the school or legal system, and individual feels unable to handle the consequences. The following listing details some notorious Schoolplace Violence incidents and their identified triggering events.

Possible Triggering Events	
John Sirola	Principal reprimand
Toby Sincino	Suspended day before (obscene hand gesture)
Jamie Rouse	Traffic accident the previous day
Evan Ramsey	Disciplinary action (principal)
Luke Woodham	Girlfriend ended their relationship
Mitchell Johnson	Girlfriend ended their relationship
Kip Kinkel	Expelled one day prior (gun possession)
Eric Harris	Rejected by military 5 days prior, turned down by three potential prom dates; Hitler's birthday
TJ Solomon	Girlfriend ended their relationship

Other Schoolplace Violence incidents may serve as triggering events in accordance with the **copycat** phenomenon. This was apparent after Columbine when several potential incidents involving bomb threats were averted. Adolescents are particularly vulnerable to the effects of social learning as repeatedly evidenced by the increase in youth suicides following the suicide of one young person. A similar trend applies in observed patterns of Schoolplace Violence. If a Schoolplace Violence incident is going to be a triggering event for others, this will usually be seen within a relatively short amount of time. The critical period ranges from 24 hours to two or three weeks following the triggering Schoolplace Violence incident. **During this timeframe, school systems should be hypervigilent to warning signs and all threats should receive intense scrutiny.**

It is important to note that misuse of this assessment scheme can result in over or underprediction of an individual's potential for violence. School personnel are advised to use **T-R-A-I-T-S** to obtain only a *preliminary* estimate of violence potential. There is a temptation to overidentify individuals as violent, and several factors need to be considered prior to any determination. These include the context of a threat, the student's past history, the total number of warning signs as well as analysis of the frequency and intensity patterns. Additionally, whenever there is serious concern based on any number of variables, an accurate profiling of a subject's lethality risk must be conducted by an individual who has expertise in these types of evaluations. And, of course, with such high stakes, exhaustive efforts to seek out the most qualified personnel must be undertaken.

After Columbine

CHAPTER FOUR

THREATS: AN IMPORTANT WARNING SIGN

The first level of violence assessment centers around analyzing threats. Of the students who perpetrated Schoolplace Violence, 93% are known to have made some type of threat, and most made more than one. All threats should be taken seriously. A good model to emulate is that of the airline industry. Airport security personnel address all threats with equal vigor, and enforces a policy of **Zero Tolerance.** School systems should adopt a similar philosophy. At a minimum, threats in schools need to be investigated, the perpetrator needs to be confronted, and the results need to be carefully documented. Schools that have already implemented this policy are seeing results. After the Kinkel shooting in Springfield, Oregon, for example, a 14-year-old boy was heard making plans to go to the school and shoot everyone. Witnesses reported seeing him make hand gestures simulating shooting people while on the school bus. He was charged with disorderly conduct and harassment, and disaster was likely averted.

Many schools have been struggling with the appropriate level of consequences for a student who makes a threat. At one school described in Newsweek (May 3, 1999), an 8th grade girl passed a note to a friend about another classmate who bothered her. She described the despised classmate as, "an ugly, flatchested ho, and I aught to kill her " (sic). A juvenile court judge took this threat seriously. The girl was convicted of third degree "terroristic threatening" and sentenced to six months probation. Too severe? Well, one needs to consider the message that is sent when a school takes such action, which on the surface may seem harsh. The goal here is to deter acts of violence. When a school system takes forceful action, a strong and clear message is sent…"That type of behavior is not tolerated here." This action could deter not only this perpetrator, but other potential perpetrators as well. It also serves to promote a sense of safety for other students and school employees. This can help develop a culture where individuals will feel comfortable disclosing threats and concerns to the proper authorities. If threats are not dealt with in this manner, the message is one of fear and apathy. Failure to confront threats in a direct and forceful manner also reinforces the perpetrator. They are empowered by manipulating and intimidating others as the targets withdraw.

Another benefit derived from a zero-tolerance policy is that the perpetrator's behavior in light of such a policy can help identify the level of severity of the threat. For instance, what is learned about the student who makes a threat in an environment where threats are not allowed? They may have impulse control problems. They may be trying to manipulate or intimidate others. They may be defiant of rules, enjoy pushing the limits, or they may be sending a cry for help. In any event, the motivations are not positive. What if the student continues to make threats after being warned to stop? Much more is now known. This blatantly defiant behavior is evidence that the student does not care about consequences, and likely has strong intentions to commit violence. At this point, significant deterrents need to be implemented.

While it is reasonable to expect that most school districts will handle threats on a case-by-case basis, it is important to strive for consistency in application of the threat policy. Inconsistent application could contribute to other potential perpetrators' perception of unfair treatment by school officials. This could fuel an individual's perceived injustice perspective and, as a result, school officials may be targeted.

Threats should always be analyzed for credibility and seriousness, and the lethality of the student assessed. While most threats are probably harmless, perhaps the result of the student "not thinking", they still need to be taken seriously. Threats can be non-verbal, verbal or written. They fall into three categories: Direct, Conditional and Veiled.

CATEGORIES OF THREATS

Direct Threats

A direct threat is a clear statement of intention to harm someone. There is no ambiguity or doubt in the statement. Examples are, "I'm going to kill you," or "I'm going to blow them away." A direct threat is punishable by law and the authorities should *always* be contacted in these instances. An example of this type of threat, that occurred in an actual Schoolplace Violence episode is, "I'm going to kill every girl who ever broke up with me." Individuals who make detailed threats that identify specific targets are more likely to become violent than those who make vague or non-specific threats. Generally, the more specific the threat, the greater the risk. This is because a high level of detail indicates the individual has spent time and effort contemplating the situation. They have likely fantasized about it and visualized the exact circumstances. Therefore, immediate action should be taken whenever a threat identifies a specific weapon, the name of the target or targets, or a time or place.

Before the Columbine massacre, Eric Harris made numerous threats on his website. He made a direct threat against a fellow student, Brooks Brown. Harris wrote, "Dead people cant do many things, like argue, whine bitch, complain, narc, rat out, criticize, or even f--- talk, So that's the only way to solve arguments with all you f---heads out there, I kill! God I cant wait till I can kill you people...especially a few people. Like Brooks Brown." Other threats by Harris were more general, "You all better f---- hide in your houses because im comin for EVERYONE soon, and I WILL be armed to the f---- teeth and I WILL shoot to kill and I WILL f---- KILL EVERYTHING!" Even when no specific targets are identified, direct threats are always cause for concern and always warrant action.

Conditional Threats

A conditional threat is one that is made contingent on time and/or action by others. Conditional threats contain the word "if," and/or the word "or." These types of threats are designed to manipulate or intimidate the target into compliance. Examples include, "You better do this **or** you're dead," and, "**If** you don't give me what I want, you will pay." Kip Kinkel made a conditional threat when he told a friend, "If I ever get really mad, I'd go and hit the cafeteria with my .22. I have lots more rounds for my .22 than my 9, and I will save one for myself." Eric Harris also made several conditional threats such as, "If you got a problem with my thoughts, come tell me and ill kill you" and "I am the law, if you don't like it, you die." He made several conditional threats against the students who ruled the school. For example, he wrote, "YOU KNOW WHAT I HATE? When there is a group of a----- standing in the middle of a hallway or walkway, and they are just STANDING there talking and blocking my f----- way!!!!! Get the f— outa the way or ill bring a friggin sawed-off shotgun to your house and blow your snotty a—head off!!" and "YOU KNOW WHAT I HATE!!!? A---- THAT CUT!!!!! Why the f--- cant you wait like every other human on earth does....If that happens one more time I will have to start referring to the Anarchists cookbook (bomb section)."

If these threats are not met with resistance and clear intolerance, they are powerfully reinforced and the perpetrator will probably continue to use them. The threat maker gets people to do things, or he derives satisfaction from seeing the recipient(s) squirm. The power gained from conditional threats can be very intoxicating. In cases of workplace violence, it has often been noted that before the perpetrator became violent he had an incredible degree of power within the company. People often reported feeling as though they were "walking on eggshells" around the individual, and worked to stay out of his way. The perpetrator senses his influence on others, and this power continues to grow unless sufficient impediments are placed in the way.

Veiled Threats

Veiled threats are the hardest type to address because they are often vague and subject to interpretation. These types of threats are very real for the recipients, but tend to lose their impact when repeated to others. The perpetrator easily minimizes this type of threat, as they refute the receiver's interpretation. The perpetrator can blame the reporter, saying the comment was taken out of context, blown out of proportion, or that it was only intended as a joke. An example of a veiled threat is the student who says, "I can see how something like Columbine could happen. I'm surprised more kids don't go off the edge." Another example is when Kinkel referred to "doing something crazy tomorrow," the day before committing Schoolplace Violence. Veiled threats are the most difficult to detect due to their vagueness and multiple interpretations. Therefore, the overall context and multiple signs are important when deciphering their significance.

With veiled threats, it is important to teach individuals the importance of attending to their feelings about a situation. The human survival instinct of fear is too often disregarded, sometimes with disastrous consequences. Too often, people talk themselves out of their feelings because they do not want to appear stupid or paranoid. In other cases, they are overwhelmed with fear of the possibility of real danger. Human beings possess fairly accurate instincts when it comes to detecting danger in the environment, but the socialization process often trains us to disregard or rationalize our gut reactions. Students and staff need to be re-trained to listen to this signal and report their concerns. There have been numerous instances after a violent incident had occurred, where individuals reflected on perpetrator's comments or actions that made them uncomfortable, but they did not know they were dealing with veiled threats.

By the time threats reach the attention of school authorities, the risk level is significant. Case studies indicate that school officials are usually the last people to know about a potential threat or even the prevalence of weapons in their school. The following newspaper excerpt is an example of this:

Attorney General Heidi Heitkamp of South Dakota reported that she asked children at a school assembly to stand up if they had ever seen anyone in school with a gun. *"Every kid in school stood up. Not one of them had ever reported (seeing) a gun in school"*

-Denver Post, July 16, 1998

In some incidents, threats are identified, but the intervention is insufficient. On the day before the shooting, Kip Kinkel was suspended for having a gun in his locker. However, no action was taken to insure that he did not return to the school, which of course he did. This case illustrates the importance of developing and implementing a standard policy and procedure for handling threatening situations. Equally as important is establishing a procedure for investigating all threats. Many institutions have adopted a **"zero tolerance policy"** regarding threats, and this appears to be the most prudent course of action. Zero tolerance means that all threats will be investigated and followed by appropriate consequences, and that threats to kill or assault others will result in a police report, suspension/expulsion, or some other type of disciplinary action. If appropriate, immediate psychological evaluation and intervention should be provided in these cases.

The FBI recommends that schools establish an anonymous, 24-hour "tip line" where students can report threats and other concerns of violence without fear of retaliation. Teachers should also be trained to identify threats and report concerns to someone in authority. In many cases, Schoolplace Violence perpetrators wrote papers, or made videos related to their violent thoughts for class projects, and these turned out to be veiled threats that were missed. At a minimum, all threats should be documented and investigated, including confrontation of the alleged maker of the statement. Additionally, it is of crucial importance that all threats be reported *verbatim*, since the exact wording and details provide insight into the perpetrator's state of mind, the lethality of the threat and potential dangerousness.

CHAPTER FIVE

PROFILING OF SCHOOLPLACE VIOLENCE PERPETRATORS

Behavioral analysis of individuals with a propensity for violence entails a thorough assessment of numerous variables, as well as aspects of the person's life. Personality traits, innate temperament, violent characteristics, habits, and exposure to violence (real or dramatized) can influence future behavior. Schools should organize a team of school-related and outside professionals with specialized training to determine the level of risk. The *"psychological profile"* of a potentially violent student includes one or more warning signs of future behavior. Each risk factor should be evaluated individually and, because student violence is always the result of several variables, multiple sources of information should be obtained prior to determining an overall rating of violence risk. If a careful and competent assessment is not performed, the novice runs the risk of underestimating a student's violence potential. Since the causes of violence in adolescents are so varied, one standard "profile" of violent offenders is unlikely to be very accurate or helpful. The following is a list of variables associated with violence potential, both general and specific to Schoolplace Violence. It should be noted that this list is neither comprehensive nor exhaustive. A competent professional who specializes in the area of violence prediction should be consulted to make formal determination of dangerousness.

The following sections outline both general indicators of violence and specific factors associated with Schoolplace Violence perpetrators. While there is some overlap, many of the General Indicators were not evidenced in all Schoolplace Violence perpetrators. However, they should still be considered when evaluating violence risk.

The reason for this is, at this time, the number of Schoolplace Violence perpetrators is statistically small. Thus, patterns established with only a minimal amount of data may not prove to be reliable over time. The following general indicators of violence have been empirically tested, and have shown a strong correlation with violence over time. While there is not a single variable capable of predicting violence, in the absence of disconfirming evidence, there is an assumption that the profile characteristics are additive. That is, the more traits or behaviors an individual evidences, the greater the probability he will act violently.

GENERAL INDICATORS OF VIOLENCE POTENTIAL

History of Violence
An old adage states, "Past behavior is the best indicator of future behavior." This holds true with violent behavior as well. The probability of future violence increases with each prior violent act. Seriously violent children and adolescents often have histories that include mutilation, torture and killing of animals. Research also indicates that children repeatedly exposed to violence are at increased risk to perpetrate violence. Some of the Schoolplace Violence perpetrators either were victims of family or peer violence, or had witnessed violence in their homes. Interestingly, very few of these perpetrators had a history of extreme violence against people. However, evidence of more low-level violence and perhaps "practicing behaviors" was present. Mitchell Johnson had pulled a knife on another student. Kip Kinkel and Luke Woodham were known to torture animals. Eric Harris and Dylan Klebold destroyed property. Many were verbally aggressive and threatening towards others, in person or on the Internet. A surprising but consistent finding is that the Schoolplace Violence incidents were usually the first time these students were physically aggressive against other people.

Poor Impulse Control
In Schoolplace Violence incidents, the violent actions were often heralded by a deterioration of the individual's impulse control system. One of the developmental tasks of childhood is the manifestation and fortification of a reasonable inhibition process for unacceptable social

behaviors. By nature, younger children have less capacity for impulse control since these systems are not yet well developed. The student who demonstrates difficulty controlling his or her emotions and behaviors in everyday situations, however, may be at risk for future violence. This particular factor is complicated by childhood disorders which affect impulse control, such as Attention Deficit Hyperactivity Disorder and Conduct Disorder. For most of the Schoolplace Violence perpetrators, the violence was a seemingly impulsive act that followed a personally significant triggering event. For others, the assault was carefully and methodically planned for some time.

Unsuccessful Personal History

A student who has repeated failures within the academic setting may be at risk for developing a low self-esteem. A person whose life is filled with failures, unattained goals, rejections, and unfulfilled dreams may choose antisocial avenues to reconcile the imbalance they feel in their life. The Schoolplace Violence perpetrators had wide variations in their academic abilities. However, almost all showed a decline in classroom performance in the weeks or months preceding the attack. Gary "Scott" Pennington, Barry Loukaitais, Luke Woodham, Eric Harris, and Dylan Klebold were all honor or above average students. Mitchell Johnson and Drew Golden were average students. Andrew Wurst was the only one described as a poor student. Apparently, academic success did not lead these perpetrators to feeling successful. In fact, being smart may have exacerbated their feelings of isolation. Loukaitis was taunted by peers for being a "nerd."

All of the Schoolplace Violence perpetrators were socially isolated, or prone to interpersonal friction with peers. Several had recently been rejected by their girlfriends. In many cases, peers teased the Schoolplace Violence perpetrators by labeling them homosexual. This was the case for Eric Harris and Dylan Klebold because they spent so much time together. Harris was described as a loner, but Klebold had several friends from a variety of social circles. After joining forces with Harris, however, the two socialized almost exclusively with each other. Both Harris and Klebold had trouble getting dates. Harris was reportedly turned down three times in his quest for a prom date. Interestingly, it is

61

suspected Harris and Klebold they planted some of their bombs during the after-prom party that was held one week prior to the massacre.

Perceived Injustice History
A perceived injustice history was evidenced by several Schoolplace Violence offenders prior to their attacks. They engaged in a great deal of blaming behavior and rarely, if ever, accepted responsibility for their life situation. Targets included siblings, classmates, teachers, principals, parents, and students. They appeared to find validation in their self-identification as a victim in an unfair world. A student with an injustice history may resort to violence as a means of retaliation and revenge. The motivation for four of the Schoolplace Violence perpetrators appeared to be revenge against principals or teachers who had disciplined them.

Obsession
Many of the Schoolplace Violence perpetrators manifested obsessive thought qualities as they became fixated on another person, persons or specific material, which was eventually evidenced in the crime. The object of the obsession may be other people, or it may be media such as music. Eric Harris and Dylan Klebold appeared to be obsessed with Adolf Hitler. They purposefully planned the massacre at Columbine to coincide with the 110th anniversary of Hitler's birth. They were known to cheer each other by yelling "Heil Hitler" during bowling matches. Harris also seemed obsessed with the video game Doom, spending countless hours perfecting his performance.

Substance Abuse
Alcohol or drugs can interfere dramatically with reasoning ability, inhibition, anticipation of consequences, and the judgement to distinguish right from wrong. Alcohol has repeatedly been shown to have a strong link to violence. However, none of the Schoolplace Violence perpetrators was intoxicated during the rampage. Dylan Klebold's nickname was VoDkA, in association with his drinking binges. But on April 20th 1999, Klebold was sober. In fact, while some of the Schoolplace Violence perpetrators abused alcohol and marijuana on occasion, but none of them had significant problems with substance abuse. While substance abuse does not appear to have a direct link to

Schoolplace Violence, it is always a consideration due to the disinhibiting effects of alcohol and drugs.

Fascination/Proficiency with Weapons
Extreme fascination with weapons, extensive gun collections, and shooting skills are indicators to consider when assessing the potential for violence. The student who continually discusses or carries weapons, or evidences an unusual enthusiasm for semi-automatic or automatic guns presents a greater risk. This type of obsession may also apply to other forms of destruction, such as explosives and bombs. A 1997 Center for Disease Control (CDC) study found that 28% of adolescent boys had carried a weapon (e.g., gun, knife or club) in the last month. Thirteen percent had brought a weapon to school in the last month. Even more startling statistics were collected by PRIDE, a respected drug-intervention program. This survey found that nearly one million school kids, grades 6 through 12, brought a gun to school last year. Almost half of the students who carried a gun to school did it often, six or more times during the year.

Drew Golden had expressed a strong interest in weapons since early childhood. T.J. Solomon became noticeably animated and enthusiastic when talking about guns. Kip Kinkel boasted about owning a butterfly knife and had told friends that he wanted to get a hook knife. This knife allows for easy maneuvering in the fist so the attacker can punch and then gouge the victim. Several of the perpetrators had shown off their weapons to friends before the incident. A significant percentage of the weapons used in the shootings were obtained from the perpetrators' homes, or the homes of relatives. Eric Harris dispersed instructions on making a pipe bomb over the Internet.

Early Onset Personality Disorders
According the diagnostic manual used by psychologists (DSM-IV, 1994), a person under age 18 can not be officially diagnosed with a personality disorder. However, personality disorders are by definition, maladaptive patterns of behavior that become deeply engrained in the individual over time. Therefore, early warning signs of personality and emotional difficulties can be identified in childhood. Some early indications of antisocial tendencies include excessive lying, fire setting,

bedwetting, and cruelty to animals. Socialization problems are evident at young ages as these children have difficulty playing with others and establishing positive relationships. They often harbor and demonstrate intense feelings of resentment for siblings. Antisocial and narcissistic features are prevalent among Schoolplace Violence perpetrators. This seems logical when one considers that development of narcissistic personality traits is a defense mechanism against feelings of worthlessness and inferiority. Antisocial behaviors serve to keep others at a distance, sheltering the individual from the risk of rejection. Narcissistic and grandiose traits were evidenced in some aspects of the plan devised by Harris and Klebold. They reportedly had a plan to kill 500 people at the school and in the surrounding neighborhood, and then hi-jack an airplane to crash into New York City. In reality, they never left Columbine High School.

Mental Illness
Major mental disorders are characterized by a loss of contact with reality manifested in delusions, hallucinations, irrational and bizarre thought processes. None of the Schoolplace Violence perpetrators had received a formal diagnosis of a severe mental illness prior to the assault. However, some had been referred for psychiatric treatment for depression. Kip Kinkel had been on antidepressants. Eric Harris had been on an antidepressant medication to decrease his obsessive thoughts and control his anger. While Schoolplace Violence perpetrators may not meet the diagnostic criteria for a severe mental illness, they certainly exist in the shadows. They may not be clinically paranoid, but they are very suspicious and rigid, and prone to all-or-nothing thinking.

After the shootings, many of the perpetrators were labeled as depressed. In most cases this was not identified prior to the violence. This could be because adolescents do not display the same depressive symptoms as adults. Rather, their distress is manifested in irritability, mood swings, isolation, temper outbursts, opposition and defiance, and excessive risk-taking. At this time, estimates for depression in American teenagers are as high as 1 out of 20. The following lists depressive symptoms typically seen in adolescents and younger children:

- Difficulty Maintaining Relationships
- Decreased Physical Activity
- Morbid or Suicidal Thoughts
- Low Self-Esteem
- Self-destructive Behavior
- Behavioral and Academic Problems at School
- Changes in Sleeping and Eating Patterns
- Frequent Complaints of Vague Physical Symptoms
- A Sad Appearance and/or Frequent Crying Spells
- Low Tolerance for Frustration
- Loss of Pleasure in Activities
- Tendency to Portray the World as Bleak or Hopeless

Preoccupation with Violence
If a student has a preoccupation with violence, it will be evidenced in almost every facet of their life. They will frequently bring it up in conversation, write about it for school assignments, and pursue it through extracurricular activities such as video games and the Internet. They will find ways to expose themselves to further violence. Examples of this could include violent musical lyrics (e.g. Marilyn Manson), movies (e.g., "The Basketball Diaries," and "Natural Born Killers"), the Internet, books and other media. Evidence of a severe preoccupation or fascination with violence is a serious risk factor for future violence. This continual exposure to violence results in desensitization and can erode inhibitions to commit violence. Their ability to generate pro-social solutions to their problems diminishes as they are inundated with violent messages.

Life Context and other Situational Variables
It is important to examine an individual's overall "life context" when assessing potential for violence. Specifically, the number of "psychological anchors," or reasons not to commit violence, need to be assessed. Factors to consider include:

- **Family Stability and Stressors**: parental conflict, domestic violence, divorce, alcohol and substance abuse or dependence, sibling rivalry, poor supervision and parental neglect

- **Major Lifestyle Changes/Disruptions**: recent moves, running away, out of home placement or threat of foster care
- **Inadequate Social Support:** deviant peer groups, few friends, socially isolated
- **Medical or Neurological Disorders:** Organic Brain Syndrome, frontal lobe damage
- **Perceived Limited Future Opportunities**: rejected from military/college, poor grades, employment difficulties
- **Lack of Positive Role-Models:** estranged and/or dysfunctional family members, lack of religious affiliations

FBI CUMULATIVE OFFENDER PROFILE

The FBI often develops a "profile" of shared characteristics among perpetrators. From this information, possible motivations are identified and the perpetrator's psychological make-up emerges. Understanding the motives of the criminals can aid investigators in predicting future crime trends. In 1998, the FBI developed an offender profile for Schoolplace Violence perpetrators. However, the FBI cautions against using this exclusively as a measure of violence risk potential, since the nature of Schoolplace Violence perpetrators may still be changing. The FBI offers the following, "The listed factors may be indicators of potentially devastating violent acts, but they are by no means certain or present in every case." The FBI profile characteristics are listed on the following page:

CUMULATIVE OFFENDER PROFILE:
SCHOOLPLACE VIOLENCE PERPETRATOR

- Indicators of low self-esteem
- Cruelty to animals; Fascination with firearms or explosives
- Mother or other family member disrespects them
- Violence only alternative used in most instances.
- Planned activity – as indicated by statements made prior to the act
- White male, 17 years of age or younger, lacks discipline
- Seeks to defend narcissistic view or favorable beliefs about self
- Depressed suicidal ideations turned homicidal by precipitating event; i.e. failed romantic relationship; lack of support from family; rejection; motive of revenge
- Acquires firearm/weapon from home; generally owned by a family member
- Perceives he is different from others; dislikes those who are different
- History of expressed anger or minor acts of aggressive physical contact at school
- May perceive a troubled relationship with parental figures though no apparent evidence of parental abuse exists
- Exhibits no remorse or flat affect (emotions) subsequent to the killings
- May have been influenced by satanic or cult type belief system or philosophy texts
- May listen to music lyrics that promote violence
- May be described as an average student
- May appear sloppy or unkempt in dress
- May be influenced by other students to commit an extreme act of violence
- May be described as isolated from others; seeking notoriety; attempting to "copy-cat" other school shooting incidents but attempting to do it "better" than the last offender
- May have a history of mental health treatment
- May have propensity to dislike popular students or students who bully others
- May have expressed an interest in previous school shooting/killing incidents
- May feel powerless, may commit an act of violence to assert power over others
- May have openly expressed a desire to kill others

While most Schoolplace Violence perpetrators are in the age range of 13 to 18, younger children may also engage in Schoolplace Violence behaviors. In these instances, they evidence the same dynamics and motives as older perpetrators. Some examples are as follows:

- In March of 1998, an eight-year old Indianapolis student sought revenge on a female student who had teased him about his ears. He brought a loaded .25 caliber pistol to school and pointed the gun at a classmate. The eight-year-old had taken the gun from his teenage brother.

- In May, 1998, in Memphis, Tennessee, a five year-old student brought a loaded .25 caliber pistol to school. He had taken the gun from his grandfather's bedroom dresser. He presented a bullet to a fellow student and said he wanted to shoot the teacher and another student. The kindergartener was allegedly seeking revenge against his teacher who gave him a "time-out."

- Just a few weeks later, on May 22, 1998, a 10-year-old student allegedly brought a loaded .25 caliber semi-automatic pistol to school, pointed the gun at a classmate's head, and said, "Pow." The student had apparently stolen the gun from under the front seat of his father's truck and brought it to school in his backpack.

One final note regarding detection of warning signs of potential violence. Due to the violent subcultures that permeate today's society, indicators of violence potential can be diluted when contrasted against such a dark backdrop. There is a significant risk that indicators of violence potential can be lost or passed over. Consideration of the context within which evaluations are conducted is crucial to an accurate violence risk assessment. There is always a significant risk that perpetrators are "hiding in plain sight."

CHAPTER SIX

PREVENTION AND INTERVENTION STRATEGIES

All schools and campus environments are at risk for violence. Most school districts have recognized the potentially devastating impact of just one violent episode and are taking a pro-active stance by developing early intervention and prevention strategies. In this process, there is a struggle for balance between overreacting and being negligent duty to protect. The reality is that a school system will never know if they overreacted, they will only know if they have under-reacted. If precautions are taken and violence never occurs, was the prevention effective in stopping the violence? Or, was the violence never going to happen in the first place? It is safe to say that most individuals, when in a position to protect children and other innocents, prefer to err on the side of caution.

Schoolplace Violence incidents can be reduced by developing and implementing policies and procedures. These guidelines are designed for early detection of potentially violent individuals, and utilization of established methods for monitoring and handling these situations. A crucial component in this strategy centers on the proper training of students, faculty and school employees. All pertinent individuals need to be educated about the dynamics of Schoolplace Violence and proven preventive measures. Training should include a message of shared responsibility among all school participants for preventing violence. Students who exhibit unusual, bizarre, or threatening behavior should be closely watched for signs of escalation and violence. Students who are volatile, extremely oppositional, evidence low impulse control, threaten and/or engage in frequent physical altercations, should not be ignored. They may be signaling a propensity toward violent behavior.

STRIKING A BALANCE BETWEEN NAIVETE AND PARANOIA

The mere thought of a violent massacre occurring at one's school is distressing. This results in one of two responses: naivete or paranoia. Naïve responders prefer to believe in the inherent goodness of people, and want to instill values of tolerance and acceptance. These responders are likely to believe that if they do not talk about or acknowledge Schoolplace Violence incidents, they will not happen again. Unfortunately, the data does not bear this out. Schoolplace Violence incidents are continuing to occur at an alarming rate and appear to be gaining momentum in both frequency and severity. The reality is that statistics are irrelevant if it happens at your school. The naïve approach creates a situation where people place themselves in potentially dangerous situations without the awareness or skills to keep themselves safe. By contrast, paranoid responders are overly sensitive to the dangers of the world, and may overreact to perceived dangers, suspending and expelling students unnecessarily. They may prefer to keep their school in continual lock-down. Individuals under the guidance of these paranoid types may become immobilized with fear.

Given the noted trend toward increased Schoolplace Violence incidents, violence preparation is becoming as important as fire prevention or other disaster preparedness. Each school community will need to assess their risk and decide for themselves where they fall on the continuum. They will need to determine the prevention strategies and interventions that best fit their culture. A good rule to follow is that "an ounce of prevention is worth a pound of cure."

The prevention and intervention strategies listed below can assist schools in developing a standard operating guide to respond to the threat of Schoolplace Violence. Many schools have implemented these and other techniques with positive response. Of course, it is understood there is no way to absolutely guarantee safety. If an individual is determined to commit violence, they will find a way. However, the laws of human behavior dictate that the more obstacles that are placed in the way, the better the chances of a successful determent. Schools should adopt the analogy of "putting up fences" to violence. Every school needs a fence, but how extensive that fence is has to be decided on a case-by-case basis. Will the school choose a white picket fence, a split-rail fence, a chain link fence, or a 20-foot electric fence topped with barbed wire?

Fortunately, most individuals who commit violence, like most suicidal individuals, have some degree of ambivalence. A good illustration of this is the recent Schoolplace Violence incident outside of Atlanta. The perpetrator had access to high-powered rifles, yet chose a low-powered one. He was an excellent shot, yet aimed low. He surrendered at the first opportunity. His actions indicate that he was ambivalent over committing violence. When effective prevention and intervention techniques are in place, there is a greater likelihood that violence will be deterred. The ambivalence will be met with resistance.

PREPARATION

Given the series of recent events, all school administrators should entertain the possibility of violence striking in their school, and develop a procedure to handle problems as they arise. To do otherwise would be naive and potentially negligent. Every school should anticipate, plan and formulate strategies for preventing Schoolplace Violence. Interventions must happen at every level. District-wide plans must intertwine and support individual school safety plans. This includes modifying existing procedures for handling traditional-type violence, as well as adding new policies specific to Schoolplace Violence. To prevent Schoolplace Violence, a standard procedure must be in place to identify students who are at risk for committing violence. A thorough plan to meet their needs, as well as defuse the situation, should be clearly and firmly established.

Develop a Threat Management and Violence Risk Assessment Team

Successful violence prevention depends on establishing a group of people to serve as a Threat Management and Violence Risk Assessment Team. This team will be responsible for evaluating threats, assessing the violence risk level and determining the course of intervention. This team should include at least one individual trained in evaluation and intervention strategies of potentially violent situations. As needed, the team could consult with outside individuals who specialize in policy development, media and public relations. Schools should be selective in choosing the representatives. Examples of potential team members include:

- Principal
- Teachers
- Local law enforcement/School Resource Officers
- Legal advisors
- Students
- Parents
- Campus Security
- School psychologists
- Professional Violence Consultant

The Threat Management and Violence Risk Assessment Team is responsible for making critical decisions quickly. All threats will be reported to the team, and they will determine the violence risk level and make recommendations regarding intervention. Other responsibilities include:

- Evaluating potential violence problems and threatening situations
- Devising and implementing intervention techniques
- Establishing a plan for the protection of students, staff, and potential targets
- Providing affected parties such as victims, families, employees, media, government, or law enforcement/rescue personnel with appropriate services
- Accessing victim assistance and community service programs
- Managing referrals for immediate and long-term counseling and treatment services

The team must work in conjunction with local law enforcement to prevent misunderstandings at the time of crisis. Authority and jurisdiction issues must be determined in advance. Specifically, when a school is in a siege situation, law enforcement officials should be the incident commanders and assume authority. The scope of additional group responsibilities and tasks for individual group members should be assigned in advance.

A central communication center or "nexus" should be established in order to provide a knowledge base for all investigations. The National School Safety Center suggests that each district develop a mandatory incident reporting system. A standard reporting form and procedure will help ensure that reporting is complete and contains consistent information. This system organizes all incidents of violence by keeping record of the details of the incident, interventions and outcomes. Any consultations, referrals or other outside intervention should also be noted in these files. This documentation will help investigators determine behavioral patterns in perpetrators, identify targets, potential means of violence, and other factors in their risk assessment.

In addition to documentation of critical or threatening incidents, the nexus can also be a resource center for those concerned with violence prevention. The communication can serve as a "clearinghouse" to distribute current literature and data on school safety issues. The center can also maintain a list of local and national experts, and others who can provide solutions to school violence problems.

POLICY DEVELOPMENT

The National Educational Service purports, "Good policies prevent problems before they occur and can help mitigate problems once they emerge." Policies reduce the chance factors in school operations by establishing a common body of knowledge. Schools that develop a "Standard Operating Guide" before it is needed are more likely to avoid panic and disruption when incidents arise. These policies should be considered highly malleable. They will be subject to change as events unfold and improvements become necessary. In addition, all school policies should be reviewed by appropriate legal counsel prior to implementation. A violence prevention policy is most effective when it is created, implemented, managed and evaluated by those who are directly involved with such assessments on a regular basis. A code of expected conduct and a standard operating guide must be included in

this prevention policy. The standard operating guide should include the following information:
- Command post
- Communication procedures
- Assignments and responsibilities
- Applicable contact data
- Facility layout
- Community Resources

The National School Board Association (1993) recommends that those developing policies to prevent violence in schools consider the following questions.

POLICY DEVELOPMENT QUESTIONS

- Is content of the policy within the scope of the board authority?
- Is it consistent with local, state, and federal laws?
- Have legal references been included?
- Does it reflect good educational practice?
- Is it reasonable? (Are any requirements or prohibitions arbitrary or discriminatory?)
- Does it adequately cover the issue?
- Is it limited to one policy topic?
- Is it cross-referenced to other relevant policy topics?
- Is it consistent with the board's existing policies?
- Can it be administered?
- Is it practical in terms of administrative enforcement and budget?

Threat Policy

Create a ***written*** zero-tolerance policy that explains the position of the school on intimidating, threatening or violent behavior. Also, establish a procedure for investigating potential problems. As with most important human relations issues, an anti-violence policy requires careful analysis and review before implementation. Include only policy criteria that can be administered consistently. Key elements include:

- Commitment from the upper-level school administrators to develop and enforce the policy.
- Training for teachers on identifying and defusing problems and conflicts.
- Training for students on identifying and reporting threats.
- A strong statement by the school district prohibiting intimidation, threats, weapons, and/or violence on school property.
- Written communication to all students and school employees about the district's policy on reporting procedures.
- A system for anonymous reporting should be implemented, but language that guarantees strict confidentiality for reporting should be avoided.
- A policy should not promise to protect students or employees from physical harm since this is not absolutely possible. It is preferable to use words such as "strive" to promote and maintain a school environment free from intimidation, and threats of violence.
- Decisions regarding use of the terms "may" and "will" in the text of the policy. The word "will" can legally be enforced as a promise to act. If a complaint is received and NOT investigated, the school district could be found negligent based on this language.
- Determine consequences for threat policy violations. Suggestions include: reporting to law enforcement, suspension, expulsion, mandated counseling, community service
- Determine how the parents will be involved in the intervention. A parent conference can help communicate concerns and provide valuable information about other questionable behaviors.

The following sample policies incorporate some of the features emphasized above. Like many work places today, schools should have a well-defined and widely communicated policy against violence. This policy should be developed with suggestions from individuals who view students from a multitude of perspectives and in a variety of situations. This well-rounded approach offers the opportunity to catch the early warning signs while there is still time for effective intervention.

<u>SAMPLE :</u> THREATS AND VIOLENCE POLICY

Our policy is to strive to maintain a school environment free from intimidation, threats, or violent acts. This includes, but is not limited to: intimidating, threatening or hostile behaviors, physical abuse, vandalism, arson, sabotage, possession or use of weapons, or any other act, which, in the administration's opinion, is inappropriate to the school environment. In addition, bizarre or offensive comments regarding violent events and/or aggressive behaviors will not be tolerated.

School employees or students who feel subjected to any of the behaviors listed above should immediately report the incident to _____ [name of designated school representative(s)]. All complaints will receive prompt attention and the situation will be investigated. Based on the results of the inquiry, disciplinary action which the administration feels appropriate will be taken.

School employees or students who observe or have knowledge of violation of this policy should immediately report it to _____ [the appointed school representative(s)]. We will investigate these events and will request the cooperation of all incident-related individuals. An employee or student who believes there is a serious threat to the safety and health of others should report this concern directly to law enforcement authorities.

SAMPLE: SEARCH POLICY

As a school district, we reserve the right to conduct at any time, without notice, searches and inspections of students' personal effects and school issued property. This may include, but is not limited to, lunch boxes, thermoses, purses, lockers, desks, backpacks, sports equipment and bags, and packages brought onto school property.

Any illegal, dangerous, or unauthorized articles discovered may be taken into custody and may be turned over to law enforcement representatives. Any student who refuses to submit their property for inspection, or who is found in possession of prohibited articles or items will be subjected to disciplinary action, up to and including expulsion from the school district.

The National Educational Service suggests additional areas to consider when developing a comprehensive violence prevention policy:
- Alternative activities for young people
- Collaboration with other agencies
- Crime free school zones
- Student conduct/discipline code
- Emergency preparedness
- Home-school linkages (e.g., parent skills training, volunteer parent patrols)
- Search and seizure issues
- Security personnel in schools
- Specialized curriculum and/or training
- Weapons in school

Topics not examined within the scope of this manual are contained in the resources listed in the Bibliography section.

NOTE: *It is crucial that the district's legal counsel review this section and any policies that are designed.*

INVESTIGATION OF THREATS AND VIOLENT INCIDENTS

A formalized plan for investigation of threats or alleged incidents of violence is necessary to prevent school personnel from being caught off-guard and unprepared when a prompt response is most critical. A carefully thought-out investigative procedure helps ensure that facts about the occurrence are collected and examined in an expedient and thorough manner. A school's immediate response may defuse the situation and avoid a costly tragedy. Conversely, a misguided response may result in tragedy.

Who conducts the investigation?
The individual or individuals appointed to evaluate the threatening situation should have training in Schoolplace Violence. They must keep a neutral and objective attitude toward all parties, and have the ability to manage the investigation in a professional manner. At various points, the administration may wish to use outside experts who have knowledge and experience in evidence collection, and in conducting investigations, interviews and interrogations. An alternative is to designate appropriately trained members of the Threat Management and Violence Risk Assessment Team to conduct the investigation. The steps of planning, conducting, documenting and evaluating evidence from the investigation should be pre-determined to insure an effective, consistent and thorough risk assessment.

Plan the Investigation
Draft investigation procedures prior to conducting any actual investigation. Consistent and comprehensive inquires result when a detailed methodology is followed in each case. Multiple sources of data are essential for an accurate determination of risk level. Thus, collateral interviews, school records, legal and violence history, parent conferences, armament inventories, nature and context of threats should all be considered.

NOTE: *Due to the fact that interviews will likely be conducted with minors, it is always prudent to consult with legal counsel prior to the interview in order to obtain guidance concerning necessary parental notification and parents' right to be present during the interview(s). This policy should be followed with regard to both allegedly dangerous students and witnesses.*

Steps in the Investigation Process

Step #1: Develop a preliminary list of witnesses or individuals involved in, or affected by, the incident.

Step #2: Specify the sequence of interviews and appoint interviewers.

Step #3: Determine what evidence the investigator can obtain for the investigation.

Step #4: Decide what, if any, action is necessary before beginning the investigation. For example, consider implementation of security measures to protect targets and/or property, or suspension of the accused student during the investigation.

Prepare for the Interview
Take into account aspects of the physical environment and ensure privacy for each interview. It is critical that students and employees feel free to discuss the problem and their concerns.

- Determine the type of information needed from each person.
- Anticipate possible reactions or responses from the alleged perpetrator.
- Develop a list of questions in advance to ask each party. Contemplate the objective of the individual, and what information is required.

- Establish rapport; remember to be empathetic and calm since the victim may be in shock. Give the interviewee time to answer, do not be impatient.
- Direct questions to the matters related to the complaint or event, unless past patterns of this conduct have occurred in which case this history is open to questioning.
- Develop questions concerning who, what, where, when and how.
- Document what each party involved did, said or knew.
- Follow appropriate questioning techniques such as:
    - Ask open-ended questions, encouraging the individual(s) to share more information.
    - Listen to the response without interrupting the flow of details.
    - Wait until the person has completed the narrative to ask for clarification.
    - Keep each question brief and confined to one point or topic.
    - Avoid leading questions that suggest or guide the answer.
    - Keep questions simple, using words that are clear to the person being interviewed.
    - Watch for nonverbal messages, and follow up with applicable questions to confirm or revise the received impression.

Conduct the Interview
Begin the investigation with the individual who reported the occurrence. Ask for details regarding:

- What happened? What action did each party take? What did each person say? Where did it happen? Describe where the action took place.
- When did it happen? Get both the date and time of the incident.
- Who was present? List the names of any potential witnesses.
- What evidence exists to corroborate the story?
- Ask for a written statement summarizing the incident at the conclusion of the interview.

After this initial interview is completed, ask the same questions to the alleged perpetrator. Witnesses and other collaterals should be interviewed in an order appropriate to the situation.

> **NOTE:** *The investigator(s) should be careful not to guarantee absolute confidentiality about the information gathered. Witnesses must understand that if the allegations are serious, their statements could be reported to others. Assure them that the statements are treated as discreetly as is practical.*

Document the Investigation

Prepare a confidential report of the investigation findings in case of a filed charge or lawsuit. The investigative notes and statements of witnesses may be used as an official record. It is important to insure that there are no extraneous comments, opinions or statements cited as fact. Stick to the objective, verifiable data of the event and do not embellish. To compile the documentation:

- Include all actual findings and their sources.
- Keep the report as confidential as practical. Only those with a legitimate need to know should have access to the report. Make only necessary copies.
- Avoid defamation claims. Generally, defamation is the unprivileged communication to a third person of a false statement intending to harm the reputation of another. To protect against the possibility of defamation, make the findings of an investigation and other pertinent documents available only to persons having a legitimate connection to, or interest in them. Do not give secretaries, supervisors, and other personnel not directly involved in the investigation access to any of the documents. Precautions against needless publication of potentially defamatory statements minimize the exposure of the school to liability.

Evaluate the Evidence

The investigating team has an obligation to analyze the data collected and formulate a course of action. This is especially difficult when one person's word against another's is the only information available. Consultation with an outside violence assessment professional is often needed in evaluating the evidence. To consider the credibility of the allegations, ask the following questions:

- When was the complaint made? If it was not immediately reported, find out why.
- Is the complaint specific and detailed?
- Are there contradictions in the information?
- Are there things missing in the evidence that should be there? Is there any logical explanation for the missing data?
- Were there other witnesses?

To consider the credibility of the accused, and any denials, ask the following:

- Has the accused student simply made a blanket denial?
- Has the accused provided evidence that either supports or contradicts the allegations?
- Have other allegations been made about this person?
- What witnesses can the accused provide to support the denial?

Take Appropriate Action

The type of corrective action necessary depends on the severity of the incident and past practice. The more serious the allegation, the greater the need for law enforcement intervention. Failure to act can increase the liability of the school. Overly severe discipline could lead to a legal suit from the family of the accused student. When a school needs to take immediate action to deal with a problem, suspending the student provides time to investigate. As the team determines consequences, they should ask, "Do the consequences fit the infraction?" Examples are of intervention could include the following:

- Suspend student pending investigation
- Student is allowed to attend school under close supervision
- Expulsion
- Psychological evaluation and/or mandated counseling
- Legal action

> **NOTE:** *If the school plans to suspend or expel a potentially violent student, escort the student from the premises, deny the student access to the school, and take extra security precautions to impede reentry. During this critical time, there should be a concerted effort to involve the parents and/or guardians in developing plans to keep the student off school grounds.*

EMERGENCY PREPAREDNESS

In addition to policy and procedures developed to prevent violence from happening, emergency plans need to be designed as well. Each school district should develop systematic procedures for dealing with different types of crises including Schoolplace Violence. The purpose of these plans is to instruct key people on how to handle actual crisis situations in an effective and efficient manner. In developing plans, take the following factors into consideration:

- Develop a Crisis Management Kit: blueprints of the school with exit routes clearly marked, important phone numbers, current school roster, contact numbers of families, etc. Make copies of the kit to be stored in several different places to ensure they are accessible in time of crisis.
- Review available on-site safety equipment, the location and possible uses. Be sure to examine exit strategies for feasibility during a

violent incident. Most exits were designed for fire escape and not violence escape.

- Include procedures for intruders, hostage situations, and catastrophic occurrences
- Examine building, grounds and supporting areas for evacuation and concealment considerations
- Identify off-campus locations where students/personnel might be moved and triaged
- Investigate crisis transportation issues – early closings, bus schedules, traffic flow, parking, emergency vehicle access
- Establish clear communication and authority responsibilities including alternates
- Determine how to disable the bell schedule to ensure safety during a crisis
- Have the Threat Management and Violence Risk Assessment Team identify the party responsible for each portion of the emergency plan
- Develop a crisis signal system to alert staff that a violent emergency has occurred or might occur. This signal should be unique for this type of emergency. Develop a different signal to alert staff that the emergency is over.
- Develop a communication plan that will inform students, staff, parents, and the community of the school's plans in case of a Schoolplace Violence incident.
- Services are now available for establishment of a mass messaging service that will telephone up to 1,000 individual numbers within an hour, and deliver a recorded message. This service can be accessed by remote from any touch-tone telephone. This type of service could be a great aid in notifying and directing parents and family members in event of a Schoolplace Violence situation.
- Establish a location and an alternate to serve as the emergency command center
- Establish a procedure for creating a list of injured students/staff that includes their names and conditions
- Establish procedures and networks for providing supportive and counseling resources
- Determine a plan for reuniting students with their parents

- Appoint a media liaison (see Media Management in Chapter 8)
- Decide how the emergency plan will be disseminated to appropriate response plan, and how these will be managed.
- Identify conditions or situations that could interfere with the emergency isolation or geographical location, critical functions the school performs, or legal responsibilities. Evaluate the efficacy of the plan through regular "violence drills." Schedule regular reviews, as conditions and staff change.

Investigation of Near-Misses

The Threat Management and Violence Risk Assessment Team should also adopt a policy similar to the FAA, which investigates all "near-misses" or close calls. These situations consist of near violent incidents where serious violence was averted at the last moment. Even if no one was hurt, the threatening situation and how it was handled should be critically evaluated. Specifically, this type of investigation involves cases where a threat was reported and the risk was determined to be minimal, yet the individual later escalated and a disaster was thwarted by emergency intervention. Questions to consider are as follows:

NEAR-MISSES: QUESTIONS TO ASK

- Did the reporting system function as intended?
- What warning signs were missed?
- Where did the system break down?
- What improvements are necessary?
- Did the Team underestimate the potential threat? Why?
- Was adequate warning provided to suspected targets? Were any targets missed?
- What steps were implemented to deter violence?
- Are the needs of any targets and victims being addressed?
- What are the plans for continued monitoring of this situation?

PUBLIC RELATIONS

The National School Safety Center makes several recommendations for cultivating a supportive climate within the school community regarding violence prevention planning. First, schools should distribute a "School Safety" brochure to parents, school staff, and students. This brochure should outline the important issues and proposed solutions to school violence. A regular newsletter can update or augment this information. Second, a school safety fact sheet can relay information about the school district's current statistics on crime, violence and disciplinary actions. These rates can be compared with statistics from the local community to investigate any new and emerging trends. Finally, awareness campaigns and recognition awards can create a positive climate towards preventing violence on campus. Logos, slogans, and promotional items can communicate and reinforce the message of commitment to safe schooling.

CHAPTER SEVEN

ADVANCED TRAINING STRATEGIES

A crucial component in deterring Schoolplace Violence relies on individuals seeing and reporting the warning signs of potential acts of violence. In order for this to occur, students, teachers and staff need to be educated on the warning signs and possible indicators of impending violence. The training also needs to emphasize the importance of reporting suspicious behaviors to identified personnel.

FRONT-LINE PERSONNEL: TEACHERS, COACHES, COUNSELORS AND SUPPORT STAFF

Those individuals who work with students on a regular and intimate basis are key players in the early identification and prevention of student violence. Too often, the warning signs of impending violence are missed, ignored or misinterpreted by those individuals who have close daily contact with the perpetrators. An example of a missed sign, evidenced in several recent cases, is bizarre writing samples submitted by the perpetrators for class assignments. These writings revealed an intense preoccupation with death and/or destruction, and some included tales of animal torture or deviant belief systems (e.g., devil worship). Other examples of missed signs are veiled threats that are open to interpretation by the recipient. For example, Michael Carneal warned, "Something big is going to happen," but no one asked what he meant, until it became painfully and tragically obvious.

As National Education Association president Bob Chase notes, too often, schools overlook the crucial role of support staff in their prevention efforts. Support staff constitute up to 40% of the public school work force. Bus drivers, cafeteria workers, custodians, and others frequently feel powerless and uninformed when it comes to school violence. These individuals often see and hear things that would not normally come to the attention of teachers. Furthermore, because of job demands, these individuals are often at great risk for becoming victims of violence themselves. Bus drivers are a good example. They are responsible for overseeing dozens of children, and because most of the time their back is to them, they are easy targets. Bus drivers may also be privy to threatening or revealing statements made by students, since they likely do not perceive bus drivers as authority figures.

Training for front-line school personnel should minimally consist of an overview of Schoolplace Violence and should also include:

- Myths and realities of student violence
- A trend analysis –what has happened at other schools?
- Perpetrator characteristics
- Early warning signals and imminent danger signs evidenced before students become violent
- Threats
- Barriers to reporting threats and concerning behavior
- How to handle a potentially violent student
- How to handle a violent emergency

A significant portion of the training should emphasize early detection and intervention. The instruction should include:
- A description and explanation of the different categories of threats
- How to analyze the lethality and dangerousness of threats
- Steps that can prevent violence from occurring on school property

The training is best presented in conjunction with dissemination of the school's policy and procedure on violence. At the end of the training, the trainees should know to whom they report suspicions, and a general idea of what happens with reported information. A crucial aspect of the training is learning the specific steps to take at the different phases of violence: before violence occurs, when violence is imminent but has not yet occurred, and in-the-moment violence. Schoolteachers should be instructed on procedures such as class containment during a crisis. The concept of "violence drills" should be introduced and implemented.

Other training issues for front-line personnel include an understanding of the student culture and the barriers to students reporting potential indicators of impending violence. The main point here is that if the teachers are hearing about it, the situation is already very serious and requires immediate attention and investigation.

COMMUNITY INVOLVEMENT AND TRAINING

Getting this information out to parents, and other community resource people in contact with students, can be accomplished through organizations such as the PTA, community education and church groups. This training will be less in-depth as the student violence policy and procedures will not need to be covered. This type of presentation could be conducted in a 30 to 60 minute session providing the essentials of sign recognition, threat analysis and intervention strategies. School officials should seriously consider asking some community groups to join them in a partnership for school peace. Some potential allies include:

- parents and parent groups
- business leaders
- all school building staff
- student clubs and activity groups
- area youth center staff
- local community policing officers
- D.A.R.E. officers
- social service agency representatives
- juvenile probation and court staff
- fire and rescue departments
- civic club and association members
- school resource officers

- Youth church groups
- Clergy
- Local sports teams and other athletes
- Prominent local citizens

Once the alliance group is formed with all relevant participants, a needs assessment should be conducted to determine the vulnerable areas of the school, and accounts of potential problems arising within the student body. A concerted effort to educate the public as to the importance of the issue should be undertaken, along with contemplation of intervention strategies.

TRAINING STUDENTS

Training students presents a different set of challenges. They may be resistant to the training and minimize the importance of it. Student training should therefore include three main goals:

(1) Enlisting student commitment to preventing violence in their school
(2) Overcoming barriers that students have to reporting their concerns. The peer code of silence and other obstacles are included here.
(3) How to identify verbal and non-verbal threats with an emphasis on recognizing veiled threats.

The first goal, enlisting students' commitment to preventing violence, may be the most difficult to achieve. There seems to be a growing apathy and disinterest among students. Fellow classmates of T.J. Solomon were interviewed after the most recent shooting outside of Atlanta. They had heard Solomon make threats but did not report them. When asked why not, they appeared complacent and one student stated, "I mean, a lot of kid of kids say that." These reactions suggest that violence is becoming commonplace in schools to the point that it is almost expected. The first task of school systems will be to overcome this attitude and obtain a personal commitment from each student to take the necessary steps to prevent violence. A suggestion for this is to provide training packets to each student and attach a "Pledge of Commitment" to each one. This commitment should include statements that the student has participated in, and understands the training on warning signs of violence and where they should report concerns. It should also include a promise to report any indications of violence potential to appropriate personnel.

The following sections outline and define problems that have been observed in students' apprehension to report threatening behavior. By understanding these barriers, schools can design a training program to begin to break down these barriers. The training and introduction of policy and procedures should be presented to students as something being done *for them* as opposed to something being done *to them*.

Peer Code of Silence
There are numerous accounts where several students knew of a gun being brought to school, or that a student had made direct or veiled threats of violence, yet nothing was reported. A major barrier to reporting is the "peer code of silence." Students often follow this unwritten, unspoken code in which it is understood that adults, parents, and teachers are the enemy, not to be trusted with information or secrets. During the training sessions, emphasis should be placed on altering this code of silence when matters concerning life and death are presented. This pattern of conduct is going to be entrenched and resistant to outside forces. Efforts to completely dissolve it are going to be met with tough resistance. The wisest course of action is to break-down the system with information about the kinds of damage it can cause. Educating students about Victims of Chance is often a good way to do this.

Common Beliefs that are Barriers to Reporting
The following are some common notions found among students who failed to report what later was found to be blatant signals that a student was contemplating violence. These beliefs should be addressed directly in the training as follows:

Belief #1: "I don't want to get anybody in trouble."

Many students are uninformed about what happens after a report of suspected violence is made. They may view reporting another student as getting that person in trouble, instead of getting them some help. This problem is a direct result of lack of information that is easily remedied by educating students about Schoolplace Violence. They need to be told that a student who is making threats, or otherwise showing signs of impending violence needs help. The students need to know their instincts are accurate and their concern is based on something real. In terms they can understand, students should be educated about mental illness, obsession, alternatives to violence and warning signs that another student may be violent

Belief #2: "He might come after me!"

A part of the peer code of silence may revolve around fear of retribution by the offending student. While revenge is a common motive for all of the Schoolplace Violence perpetrators, there has not yet been a case where the target was a student who filed a report against them. Students should be advised that very often, the potential perpetrator is really asking for help in a disguised manner. The student should also be assured that his/her confidentiality will be protected as much as is practical. The FBI recommends a 24-hour recorded tip-line for witnesses to report threats and the existence of weapons in school. Protecting the anonymity of the reporter is up to the discretion of each school. In some instances, complete confidentiality may be impossible. In any event, individuals who have made a report of this sort feel that they have taken a great risk and may need extra protection. Any escalation of threats against the reporter after identifying a potentially violent perpetrator should be addressed immediately.

Interestingly, Harris allowed what had appeared to be a target student to go free. Brooks Brown was another Columbine student whom Harris had repeatedly threatened and harassed. Harris had told Brown directly that he was going to kill him. Brown's parents had called the police on Harris but what action was taken is unknown. As Harris was entering the school, he encountered Brown whom he told, "Brooks, I like you now, go home." There is a possibility that Harris knew of the Browns' report to the police and let Brooks go because he had in effect "stood up to him." Harris may not have been allowed to intimidate Brooks Brown, and this had somehow changed the dynamics so that Harris no longer targeted him.

Belief #3: "So what if he's violent, he won't come after me."
Denial is often used by people to ward off fears and anxieties, and this hold true for young people as well. Students may think they are good friends with the potential perpetrator, and would never be hurt by him. The reality is that in the spree-type shootings common in Schoolplace Violence incidents across the country, a friendship with the perpetrator is no guarantee of safety. Typically, the shooter is prepared to die and has few, if any, loyalties when they enter the school zone to commit the crime. During shootings, perpetrators are usually not aware of where they are shooting or at whom. The potential to be caught in the crossfire is significant. It should be made clear to the students that in many of these cases, even non-targeted individuals are at a great risk due to the spree nature of the killing. The optimal intervention to combat this type of barrier is training on Victims of Chance.

Belief #4: "I'm overreacting. This kind of thing doesn't happen here."
After almost every Schoolplace Violence incident, people inevitably say, "I never thought this would happen here." Most people do not want to believe that violence will happen to them. People are afraid that others will perceive them as paranoid if they voice their concerns. Denial and mistrusting one's instincts can play a major role in permitting violence to occur. Students should be taught to listen to their gut feelings, because their intuition about situations and people is often incredibly accurate. A good analogy is the behavior or animals in the wild that, upon detecting signals of danger, react quickly and decisively. For more information about instinct and the usefulness of fear, please see the bibliography section of this book.

The Logistics of Training
Some suggestions regarding the logistics of the training are offered in the next section. The best training location is a classroom, which is conducive to small group discussion, and a familiar environment in which to discuss emotional and often anxiety-provoking material.

Ideally, the topics of violence should be covered within an existing mandated curriculum such as a health course. The atmosphere should encourage students to speak freely. The discussion should elicit from the students their experiences, fears and attitudes towards reporting the danger signs.

The students should be provided with handouts of topics covered, along with a signature page delineating the personal responsibility of each student in preventing Schoolplace Violence. The student's signature should be obtained under an oath attesting that they have read and understand all aspects covered in the training, as well as the school's policy on threats and violence. A promissory intention by the student to dutifully report any suspected signs should also be included. The students should be assured of an intention of confidentiality for reporting their concerns and the limitations on this confidentiality.

In addition to training for high school and junior high school students, training for younger children should also take place. While this may seem alarming to some, cases of grade school and even pre-school children bringing guns to school have occurred. This training should cover basic concepts of violence and reporting procedures.

SURVIVING A VIOLENT INCIDENT

Surviving a violent incident is dictated by a basic principle of physics: action is faster than reaction. The perpetrator always has an advantage because he is one step ahead of the potential victim. This leaves the potential victim in the disadvantaged position of having to guess or wait for the perpetrator's action. While violent individuals may have the upper hand, there are several things potential victims can do to protect themselves and increase chances of survival. When potential victims are equipped with survival strategies, they become strong contenders. **Responding** is much more effective than **reacting.** When people behave impulsively, chances are they will make a decision that places them in greater danger. Performance under stress is compromised in many ways:

- *Fine motor skills become impaired.* When building a response plan for violence, it is important to rely on gross motor movements like the arms and legs rather than the fine motor movement of the fingers. When companies ask for an evaluation of their emergency response plan, a frequent criticism is the many demands that require fine motor skills. For example, many places of business have an alarm system for first line responders. The alarm triggers are sometimes difficult to reach and require a pressing a button with a finger. To initiate other alarm systems, the responder must punch in a code. Even dialing the phone requires fine motor movement. All of these behaviors are compromised under extreme stress. Alarm triggers should rely on gross motor rather than fine motor movements and emergency numbers should be pre-programmed for speed dialing.

- *Perceptions become distorted.* When individuals are under extreme stress, the rush of adrenaline causes a 20% decrease in blood flow to the brain. Some senses become acute and amplified, while others are dampened. It appears that under stress, the body channels it energy into its most favored sense. Individuals who are strongly visual will have increased visual acuity. Those with a strong auditory orientation report increased hearing ability. Additionally, the decreased blood flow to the brain causes the experience of feeling as though the world has turned into a very surreal, slow motion movie. Reality is altered. Perceptions become more distorted as people try to anticipate what will happen next. Very often objects in the environment seem larger or smaller and may even appear or disappear. An example of this stress-induced misperception occurs when a police officer makes an error in judgment. Under stress, officers make guns, knives, and other deadly objects "appear" (when the suspect is really holding something else) or "disappear" (when the officer is not suspecting danger based on their expectations in a given situation). Officers have been known to draw their weapons on suspects carrying nothing more lethal than a soda can. In that moment, the shiny metal can is interpreted as a knife. Perception becomes reality.

- *Tunnel thinking interferes with adaptive problem solving.* When people are in traumatic situations, their thinking often gets locked into one mode. For instance, in workplace violence situations, employees often attempt use the phone to call for help. They instinctively dial "911" as they have been taught their whole lives. Unfortunately, this strategy does not work in many places of business because the company phone systems require people to dial "9" first to get an outside line. Under tremendous stress, many people forget this and are caught in a loop of repeatedly dial "911."

Given the failings of human body and brain under extreme stress, schools should educate students and staff on survival tactics during a violent incident. As humans become more civilized and technologically advanced, they rely less on instinctual survival skills. In fact, many instinctive reactions are now inappropriate and possibly even dangerous. For example, think about the behavior of crowds during a fire. Often a crowd of people runs hysterically toward the nearest exit, causing a big jam. Consequently, people need to worry not only about being burned, but trampled as well. Another example of poor survival tactics in humans is running behavior. When a predator is chasing an animal in the wild, the animal attempts escape by running in a zigzag, serpentine pattern. When humans are chased they run in a straight line, giving a pursuer a distinct advantage because the travel direction is predictable.

Many schools have implemented "violence drills" that are similar to fire drills. During these drills (and the real thing) a school-wide tone signals there is someone on school grounds with a gun. The object is to get in a barricaded and safe position as quickly as possible. Inner-city schools implemented these techniques years ago, with great success. In order to survive a violent incident, people need to learn how to overcome inappropriate responses, distorted perceptions, impaired senses and motor skills, and tunnel vision. This can only be accomplished through practice and behavior rehearsal, in a fashion similar to fire drills.

NOTE: WHILE NO STRATEGIES CAN GUARANTEE SAFETY, THERE APPEARS TO BE SIGNIFICANT BENEFIT FROM PRACTICING FOR THESE EVENTS.

CHAPTER EIGHT

VIOLENCE-INDUCED TRAUMA

The trauma from a Schoolplace Violence incident, or near-incident, can be serious and have far-reaching impact as illustrated below.

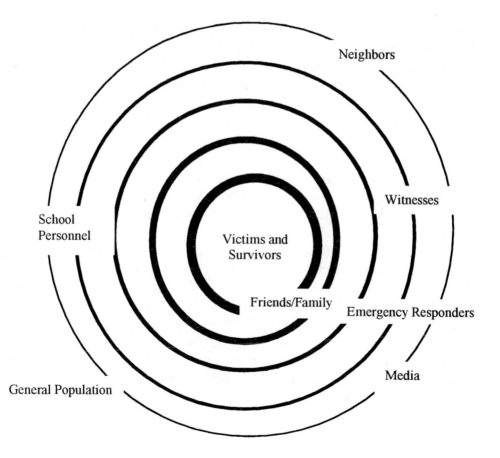

CRITICAL FACTORS FOLLOWING A VIOLENT INCIDENT

Timely intervention in incidents where violence has already occurred is key to beginning the healing process as quickly as possible. The school system's top administration, and all members of the Threat Management and Violence Risk Assessment Team are involved in the post-incident phase. They are responsible for coordinating services for victims, survivors and their families, as well as addressing the media and non-involved students and their families. These tasks can seem overwhelming during such a chaotic time. Schools that have successfully dealt with Schoolplace Violence revealed the following common themes:

Leadership and Unity
Principals, teachers, key administrative personnel, and student leaders should be highly visible and display intense personal involvement. In the aftermath of a Schoolplace Violence incident, people not directly involved begin to make assumptions about the community in which the perpetrator resided. For example, the rash of school shootings in Arkansas and Kentucky led the media to speculate about the "Southern Culture of Violence" as a contributing factor. Perceptions such as these are frequently unfounded and can be offensive and even detrimental to survivors. Leaders of the community should directly address these misattributions and send a powerful message of solidarity.

The officials at Columbine provided good examples of steps to be taken after a Schoolplace Violence incident.. Principal Frank DeAngelis was visible with his emotional reactions and repeatedly complemented the students on the way they handled themselves during the crisis. When he got to the podium at the April 25th memorial service, the crowd gave him a standing ovation and he wept. During the graduation of Columbine's class of 1999 he stated, "You are my special children, and I love each and every one of you." Columbine senior Amber Burgess spoke at the memorial service, and began the chant that unified the community, "We are Columbine! We are Columbine!"

Crisis Aftermath Task Force

In the aftermath of tragedy, a pre-arranged task force can be instrumental in addressing the needs of affected individuals. The group can facilitate communication, between the task force and those impacted, and plan and organize the many post-incident events. *All affected groups should be represented on this team: teachers, administrators, students, parents, custodial staff, and others.* This point cannot be emphasized enough. In the aftermath of the Columbine massacre, some felt that students were underrepresented in the discussions and planning that ensued.

Debriefings and Victims' Assistance

Debriefings are group discussions that incorporate education, information, and crisis intervention techniques. Typically, the composition of the groups should be somewhat homogeneous, revolving around those individuals similarly effected. For example, only those people directly involved would attend one de-briefing while there may be another for the siblings or families, another for students not directly involved, another for the community, etc. The goal of debriefings is to minimize the psychological symptoms resulting from the traumatic event. A major component in this is educating the individuals as to the "normal" course of trauma, and informing them what they can expect over the next days and weeks. The debriefings should be offered in a timely manner and follow-up debriefings may be necessary.

During the actual debriefing, the participants discuss their experience pertaining to the event, and their subsequent thoughts, reactions and any symptoms or difficulties. Each individual voicing their perceptions of the events, in a chronological order, helps all participants construct a coherent account of the incident, which often feels like a fragmented, surrealistic event. Debriefings should conclude by focusing on survivor strengths, coping skills, ways to help the healing process and things that hinder the healing.

Mental health professional should be present to facilitate discussion and educate group members about normal stress reactions, symptom management and when to seek additional help. In addition, peers may be more likely than outside experts to understand the social circumstances and organizational factors particular to the participants.

Community referrals and readings for further assistance and information should be provided as well.

In addition to debriefings, other forms of victims' assistance are appropriate and should be offered as options. Mandatory counseling under these conditions is not recommended and is likely to be counterproductive. People who are traumatized need to feel in control of their lives again and should be allowed to heal and address problems at their own rate. Schools should have already identified specific mental health providers to respond in such circumstances. Too often in post-violence situations, there is an influx of sensation or notoriety seeking "professionals." They may offer their services for free just to be part of the scene. They may show up without being invited. At the reuniting area for students and parents on the eve of the Columbine incident, "counselors" outnumbered victims and families. This is not uncommon. Following the crash of TWA Flight 800, back in July 1996, the American Red Cross announced they had gathered almost 500 volunteers, mostly mental health counselors to help families. At the same time, another welfare agency was sending their grief counselors to the airport. Once again, counselors outnumbered victims.

Crisis can attract people who are excited by the event and not always motivated by a genuine concern to help others. These individuals will likely abandon the situation when the novelty wears off. Others may purport to be experts on trauma, but not have the experience to deal with the magnitude of a Schoolplace Violence incident. They may soon realize they are in over their heads. The Emergency Support Network recommends the following steps to provide effective psychological assistance following traumatic events:

- *Plan who will provide psychological services.* These individuals may be internal or external to the school organization. Making this very important decision in the midst of a crisis can result in utilizing individuals who are inappropriate or inadequately trained or experienced.

- *Use an appropriate response time frame.* Professional mental health workers may not be needed immediately after the violent incident. Sometimes they are mistakenly called prematurely, with the expectation that this will facilitate a rapid recovery for the victims. This impulsive reaction often ignores the practical needs of both the victims and the counselors, and may even inhibit the normal crisis recovery process.

- *Practical assistance and referrals are appropriate first responses.* In the immediate aftermath of violence, victims may need mundane assistance. Instead of counseling, transportation and financial assistance may be more beneficial. For the Columbine students, many found that their cars were part of a crime scene for several days after the event. Transportation became a major issue in helping them reestablish order in their lives. Professional counseling is more likely to have a role after the immediate impact has passed, and the victims are looking for, or needing, support beyond what their friends and family can provide.

- *Provide a "menu" of services from which victims and their families can choose.* Services can include a 24-hour crisis hotline/information line, psychological debriefings, educational seminars on "Helping a victim through a trauma," post-trauma counseling, follow-up debriefings or telephone contact, and trauma-anniversary assistance.

Provide a Sense of Security

Increasing security in the weeks and months post-incident will help reassure the school community that serious efforts are being implemented to prevent tragedy from re-occurring. In the immediate aftermath of a Schoolplace Violence incident, schools are at a high risk for copycat behavior. The FBI suggests uniformed School Resource Officers be on hand to provide positive information quickly, and to weed out rumors regarding potential acts of violence. They further recommend that law enforcement officials have lunch in the schools on a regular basis in order to talk with the students and to build trust. Safety measures in the aftermath of Columbine included continuous sweeps of buildings for bombs and explosives, and review of emergency protocol. During the first few weeks after Columbine, some school districts modified dress code policies to prohibit students from wearing trench coats like those worn by the gunmen.

Constructive Outlets
Often, people can find a sense of purpose and meaning in terrible events if they can channel their sorrow or anger into action. Additionally, tangible symbols of the tragedy can provide a sense of solidarity for the community. Following the Columbine massacre, for example, several factors facilitated the grieving process.
- Immediately after news of the tragedy broke, people began standing in line for hours at blood donation sites as hospitals announced their supplies were running low.
- Blue and silver ribbons began appearing everywhere – jacket lapels, backpacks, storefronts, and media images. They became the symbol for hope and recovery.
- Monument Hill, a park adjacent to Columbine High School became a memorial site where hundreds of thousands of people from around the country came to pay their respects to the victims.
- Thousands of people attended a memorial service in downtown Denver on April 25, 1999. Songs written in memory of the victims played on local and national radio. These musical symbols of the tragedy carried a message of connection and support.
- Hundreds of banners and sympathy cards, from schools and various organizations around the world hung for public display in a mall.
- Scholarships, survivor funds, memorial gardens, foundations, and charity events to raise money for the victims gave the community a way to participate in the healing process as a unified group.

MEDIA MANAGEMENT

The media can have a positive or negative impact on the community in the aftermath of a violent tragedy. Without doubt, Schoolplace Violence incidents attract members of the press in droves. It is important to have a strategy to handle this, and to know the rights survivors have with the media. Each school should identify one spokesperson, and an alternate, to minimize confusion and contradictory statements. The

Threat Management and Violence Risk Assessment Team should have pre-established guidelines for sharing appropriate information ahead of time. Ask questions before speaking into the microphone – **interviewees are not at the mercy of the reporter**. Avoid potential distractions. Select a time and location based on comfort level of the interviewee, not the convenience of the reporter. Do not accept a cold call interview in the home, or during the normal business day. Prepare for the interview by asking what questions will be asked, and what direction the interview will take. Be honest and do not speculate. Share only factual, appropriate, and authorized information. Never say, "No comment" if the question cannot be answered. Instead, provide the reason that answer cannot be given at this time.

RIGHTS WITH THE MEDIA

- The school community has the right to grieve and recover in private

- The right to say "no" to an interview

- The right to request a specific reporter

- The right to refuse an interview with a specific reporter

- The right to speak to only one reporter at a time

- The right to refrain from answering any questions that makes the interviewee uncomfortable

- The right to ask to review quotations prior to publication

- The right to demand a retraction when inaccurate information is reported

- The right to ask that offensive photographs or visuals be omitted from airing or publication

Adapted from Slover, C. & Tasci, D (1999) Trauma Recovery Handbook, published by Nicoletti-Flater Associates

Follow-Up Services

For the most part, society responds well immediately after a crisis, but once the fanfare dies down, the victims are left wondering, "Where did everybody go?" Periodic check-in points for students, teachers, and staff will let survivors know they are supported in their continued struggle and healing. Be prepared for significant dates for the survivors: graduation, birthdays, special dances, the re-starting of school, and especially the anniversaries of the trauma (e.g., one week, one month, three months, and annual).

Evaluate the Process

After the intensity of the crisis has passed, all parties involved in the violence prevention, intervention, and aftermath should conduct a tactical de-briefing as a group. Pertinent questions are, "What worked?" and "What didn't?" The analysis and discussions of these committees should yield a report of "Lessons Learned" from the incident. The report should include recommendations to be implemented as soon as possible, and shared with others.

POST-TRAUMA RESPONSES AND THE "NORMAL" COURSE OF TRAUMA

Everyone who is victimized by a life-threatening situation, is not necessarily traumatized. Responses to emotionally intense experiences are strongly influenced by past history and personality makeup. Therefore, it is unreasonable to expect that everyone who endures the same traumatic experience will exhibit symptoms and post-trauma reactions. In fact, suggesting there is something wrong with people who are not grossly affected may prove detrimental. People should be encouraged to "feel what they are feeling." The truth is, there is no standard way to respond to extra-ordinary events, and each person will evidence an individual reaction.

Trauma Symptoms

A Schoolplace Violence incident is certainly a traumatic event and will likely cause strong physical and emotional reactions in those involved.

These aftereffects are considered, *"normal reactions to very abnormal events."* During this time, the mind and body are trying to adapt and cope with a life-threatening situation, and react with a survival mode of "Red Alert." Irrational fears, discomfort with previously enjoyed activities, worries about family members and loved ones, are examples of the unwillingness of the body and psyche to be victimized again.

In addition to this activation of survival instinct, there is the impact of shattered assumptions. All people hold assumptions about the world and ourselves. These fundamental beliefs are often not conscious, and they are quite resistant to challenge and change. According to trauma specialist Dr. Janoff-Bulman, these assumptions usually center around three themes: "The world is benevolent," "The world is meaningful," and "I am a good and worthy person." Most people believe the world is a safe and fair place, and people are moral. From these core beliefs, people derive the adaptable sense of trust, security, and invulnerability. These traits enable us to go through the day and interact with others without distress.

When a person experiences a traumatic event these assumptions are dramatically challenged and often shattered. This is especially true when traumatic events are perpetrated by another human being. Research has consistently shown that trauma inflicted by another person, as opposed to those resulting from natural disasters such as hurricanes, tornadoes and floods, are more damaging and tend to complicate and prolong recovery. The disillusionment and "depressive realism" that can stem from such events can be paralyzing. In other words, the individual's sense of trust, security and invulnerability is gone. The survivor becomes aware of the reality of surrounding danger and loss potential. The implications can be overwhelming.

In the process of trauma recovery, survivors learn to rebuild their assumptions by integrating the new traumatic experience. Talking with others, or writing about the event, is a very effective way to impose order on a chaotic event. By nature, humans are very verbal creatures, and need to put words to experiences. This is even truer for emotionally loaded incidents.

Another phenomenon associated with trauma is "survivor guilt." When survivors blame themselves for what happened, it is often in an attempt to find some degree of control over an out-of-control situation.

"If only I had done this…" or, "If only I had not done that…" or "Why did I survive when others didn't?" are statements often heard repeated by the victims of a traumatic incident. This attempt to regain control and predictability over one's life re-establishes a sense of fortitude and the belief that a person can control his/her own destiny.

Finding some benefit or purpose in the experience can also assist with the "meaning-making" process for survivors. It is important to know that the event did not happen for nothing. The benefits found often involve a rediscovered appreciation for life, one's family and loved ones, and oneself. This drive for resolution can be aided by the community activities previously discussed.

Post-Traumatic Stress Disorder **(PTSD)** is a psychological syndrome that affects individuals who have experienced a critical incident. The cluster of symptoms including nightmares, flashbacks, hyperarousal, dissociation, depression, and avoidance, was first noticed in WWI veterans returning from combat. It was initially labeled "shell shock," and then later "battle fatigue." Over the last several decades, research in the area of psychological trauma has discovered that other life-and-death situations, earthquakes, rape, domestic violence, airplane crashes, car accidents, and violent crime, can produce similar effects.

For many individuals, the symptoms gradually disappear with time, but for others, the symptoms can persist with varying intensity for decades. It is expected that the "normal" course of a traumatic reaction spans four to six weeks. In fact, an individual can not be diagnosed with PTSD until the symptoms have persisted for at least four weeks. The symptoms of PTSD fall into three categories:

1) **Intrusive Symptoms:** These symptoms occur when the images, sounds, smells, tactile or taste sensations related to the traumatic event unexpectedly "intrude" into the person's consciousness. These vivid memories may be manifested during sleep in the form of nightmares. Others are "triggered" by internal or external cues that resemble some part of the trauma. When this happens, the trauma is repeatedly re-experienced. This can be quite distressful to the individual, and one needs to understand that it is all part of the normal healing process. It is

as though the brain is searching its memory banks, looking for a similar memory or point of reference and when none is found, the trauma resurfaces as though the brain is saying, "File not found." Eventually, the brain will create a new "file folder" where this traumatic information will be stored, but this process can take several weeks. With the survivors of the Columbine massacre, re-experiencing the trauma was a common symptom. Sounds similar to the fire alarms that rang through much of the ordeal have frequently been triggers for intense anxiety responses. Many survivors have had difficulty sleeping. Some hear the bullets and bombs going off as they are falling asleep. Others wake up, "frozen, seeing Dylan and Eric's faces."

2) **Avoidance Symptoms:** Re-experiencing the traumatic event is usually painful, so many individuals develop avoidance patterns to dampen the intensity of the uncomfortable feelings. For example, an individual with PTSD may avoid situations that are reminiscent of the traumatic event. Others may become numb to emotions altogether. Depression and a loss of pleasure in life are common results of the withdrawal and "emotional shutting down" that occur. The Columbine community has struggled with the issue of avoidance. Many believe that the library, where many died, should be torn down and rebuilt. Some think the same of the entire school. The decision regarding the library will be determined by a poll of the teachers and students. Others state that they want to go back because, "If we don't, they win." Several students returned to Columbine over a month after the massacre. One student retrieved her backpack, notebooks, and locker contents and proceeded to throw them in the trash when she got home stating she "didn't want anything to do with it." The mother of the same student mentioned that her daughter avoids the streets passing the high school.

3) **Hyperarousal Symptoms:** Individuals with PTSD often demonstrate hypervigilence, as they feel constant pressure to be on guard for danger. They experience exaggerated startle responses, irrational and new fears, increased irritability, and sometimes explosive anger. They may have difficulty concentrating or remembering new information. Sleep disorders and disrupted appetite is common. The explanation for these symptoms is that some of the resources of the brain

445553345

are being drained off to process the traumatic material. Therefore, the individual is operating at a diminished capacity; the usual reserves for emotional stability are significantly decreased.

There are several associated symptoms that may be present when one develops PTSD. These include:

- Alcohol or drug abuse (attempt to "self-medicate" painful feelings)
- Anxiety and panic attacks
- Suicidal thoughts, gestures or attempts
- Extreme guilt
- Feelings of alienation or intense loneliness

If these or other symptoms persist for longer than one month, and interfere with the individual's life, professional counseling services with a therapist who is well versed in trauma should be sought.

Trauma Phases
Individuals who are traumatized proceed through different phases during the recovery process. While each person may vary widely in their clinical presentation and array of symptoms, the overall process for everyone is similar. Sometimes traumatized individuals will re-cycle through earlier stages when their traumatic experience is triggered. Others will proceed through the stages in a direct sequence. There is not necessarily a right or wrong way to go through this process, and all time parameters mentioned here are general guidelines. Some people may move quickly through the phases while others may take years to come to resolution.

1) **SHOCK**
The first phase begins at the onset of the traumatic event, and can continue for up to a week. The perceived threat of death or injury is very real. Sensory information floods the brain. Sights, smells, sounds and feelings overwhelm the individual's entire being. The brain is unable to process it all, and emotional numbness sets in. At the time of the traumatic event, there are often distortions in time and space, as well as auditory and visual misperceptions. The experience of events is in "slow motion," there is an unreal or dream-like quality to them. Sounds

may be intensified, muted or absent. Things may look different and unfamiliar, and there may be an intense focus on only one part of the visual field. There may be a strange sense of calm due to a survival mechanism of extreme denial in the presence of overwhelming danger. There may be some physical symptoms, including agitation, hyperalertness, over-activity, or biological disruption (e.g., sleeping and eating patterns).

2) IMPACT

This phase often begins when an individual leaves the location of the critical incident, and can persist from a few days to several weeks. This phase frequently triggers confusion and a sense of being overwhelmed as full realization of the extent of the danger, damage, death or injury is made conscious. The individual may become highly emotional when leaving the scene of a disaster. They will likely feel a strong need to isolate, but should be with others for support and to ensure a reconnection with people.

3) RECOVERY

This phase begins with return to a near-normal routine pattern, accompanied by stable days. There will be a decrease in the symptoms of the impact phase, and attention, concentration, reasoning ability, recall, and emotional expression gradually return. This phase often resembles an emotional roller coaster with a mixture of good days and bad days. The important thing here is stringing together good days.

4) POST-TRAUMA RESOLUTION

This phase occurs after returning to one's routine pattern. Here the trauma's impact will show longer-term changes in behavior, thought patterns, beliefs, emotions, and perception. These changes may be irreversible. There are two possible outcomes of this phase: positive resolution, or negative reaction with no resolution. The positive course will lead to acceptance of the event and the individual's actions, along with a positive re-evaluation of goals and values. Keep in mind, this may be a lengthy process. Without trauma resolution, there is a strong likelihood of a chronic struggle throughout life with distress, family problems, job difficulties, chemical dependency, and potential suicide.

Some Basic Coping Strategies

- **Education.** There are several, readily available self-help books that which describe the nature and course of post-incident trauma, and offer suggestions for treatment and intervention. Some of these are listed in the Bibliography section of this book.

- **Understand that healing occurs in stages over time.** After a traumatic event, life may not return to the way it was due to permanent losses and changes in views of the world and the self. Many assumptions about life have been destroyed, and developing a new set of beliefs will take time. Don't expect the traumatized individual to just "snap out of it."

- **Get support.** Victims, their families, and others affected by the violent incident should talk about their experiences and feelings with supportive individuals. A formal psychological debriefing could be arranged to help with this process. An on-going support group may also be helpful as this affords the opportunity to share and normalize the impact of the event. Professional counseling should be considered if the trauma is particularly severe or if symptoms continue beyond four weeks.

- **Empowerment.** After the turmoil and intense emotional processing has passed, many people find they can derive strength from the knowledge gained from the trauma. Some people volunteer to help other trauma survivors. Others write about and publish their experience. Some pursue legal avenues for compensation in order to regain a sense of control over the world.

CHAPTER NINE

THE RIPPLE EFFECTS OF COLUMBINE

The tragedy at Columbine High School has already evidenced dramatic effects on the landscape of American schooling. From all indications, these changes are likely to continue. Improvements in school security, prevention strategies, policies and procedures have already been implemented at Columbine. Some examples are:

- Security improvements: video cameras, increased lighting and security doors are installed
- Two additional campus supervisors
- Additional police agency support
- Construction of a "safe room" where students can meet with two newly hired mental health counselors
- A volunteer coordinator to ensure participation of parents and the community
- Implementation of a "call-in" system for concerns
- Funds for teachers to provide additional time and support services to students who need academic support because of stress, difficulty concentrating, entering and staying in the school, etc.
- Special services for victims and their families including: a district cabinet contact to answer questions and concerns, a dedicated call-in line for victim families, support services for siblings of victims within the school district, organization of a special orientation to Columbine for victims and their siblings
- Review and revisions of county schools' crisis plans

- Funds for programs in non-violence and safety
- Mailings provided for affected groups in the community

In addition to these proposed changes, school officials developed an elaborate scenario for welcoming students back to school on the first day. They provided tee-shirts that said "We are.....Columbine," to be worn on the first day of school. Teachers, administrators, parents, alumni and staff formed a human chain for students to pass through as they entered Columbine in an effort to "take back the school" from violence. After re-entry the school flag, which had been at half-mast since April 20th, was raised.

Despite the best efforts of school officials, the first day of school was tainted with reports of freshly painted swastikas in the restrooms. As this book goes to press, school officials are dealing with a series of threat letters sent to five district high schools that warn, "Columbine was just the beginning." These types of incidents are to be expected as they frequently occur after a violent incident of this magnitude. Examples of the copycat phenomenon, as previously outlined, were also anticipated. However, what was not expected was that the perpetrators at Columbine could influence adult workplace violence perpetrators.

Two months after Columbine, a workplace violence incident occurred in the Denver metro area that was eerily similar to Columbine. Two employees had written a threat letter that outlined their plans to detonate bombs at their workplace. In this letter, the two alleged assailants referred to the Columbine incident in an admiring manner. They distorted the positive aftermath of Columbine, the community rallying together, by implying that a tragedy like Columbine should happen more frequently. The parallels between this incident and Columbine were striking. This observation strongly suggests that the fallout from the massacre at Columbine High School has yet to be completely realized.

BIBLIOGRAPHY

The author recommends the following books and articles for further information on the topic of violence prevention, intervention and aftermath.

Violence Prevention and Intervention

American Psychological Association (1993). *Violence and youth: Psychology's response (Vol. 1).* Washington, D. C.: APA

Baron, S. (1993). *Violence in the workplace.* Ventura, California: Pathfinder Publishing.

DeBecker, G. (1999). *Protecting the Gift.* New York, New York: Random House

DeBecker, G. (1997). T*he Gift of Fear.* Boston-Toronto: Little, Brown & Co

Dwyer, K., Osher, D. & Warger, C. (1998). *Early warning, timely response: A guide to safe schools.* Washington, DC: U. S. Department of Education.

Eron, L. D., Gentry, J. H. & Schlegel, P. (Eds.). (1994). *Reason to hope: A psychological perspective on violence and youth.* Washington, DC: American Psychological Association.

Furlong, M. J. & Smith, D. C. (Eds.). (1994). *Anger, hostility, and aggression: Assessment, prevention, and intervention strategies for youth.* Brandon, VT: Clinical Psychology.

Gibbs, N. May 31, 1999. "Special Report: School Violence," Time, (33-49), NY: Time, Inc.

Guerra, N. & Tolan, P. (1994). *What works in reducing adolescent violence: An empirical review of the field (Rep. No. F-888).* Boulder: University of Colorado, Center for the Study and Prevention of Violence.

Langone, J. (1984). *Violence: Our fastest growing public health problem.* Boston-Toronto: Little, Brown & Co.

Kellerman, J. (1999). *Savage spawn: Reflections on violent children.* New York: Library of Contemporary Thought, Valentine Publishing Group.

Kinney, J. & Johnson, D. L. (1993). *Breaking point: The workplace violence epidemic and what to do about it.* Chicago, IL: National Safe Workplace Institute

Mountain States Employers Council, Inc. & Nicoletti-Flater Associates (1994). *Violence goes to work: An employer's guide.* Denver, Colorado: MSEC & NFA, Publishers.

Nicoletti, J., Spencer-Thomas, S. & Porter, K. (1998). *Survival-oriented kids in a violent world: A skills training manual for parents and other protectors.* Denver, Colorado: Nicoletti-Flater Associates, Publishers

U. S. Department of Health and Human Services (1993). *Request for assistance in preventing homicide in the workplace.* NIOSH Alert. Cincinnati, OH

VandenBos, G. R. & Bulatao, E. Q. (Eds.) (1996). *Violence on the job: Identifying risks and developing solutions.* Washington, D. C.: American Psychological Association.

Weltmann, R. Huml, F. J. (Eds.) (1998). *Ready-to-Use Violence Prevention Skills: Lessons & Activities for Secondary Students.* Prentice Hall Trade.

Violence Aftermath

Trauma Recovery (Adult)
Herman, J. L. (1997). *Trauma and recovery.* New York: Basic Books

Janoff-Bulman, R. (1992). *Shattered assumptions: Towards a new psychology of trauma.* New York: The Free Press.

Matsakis, A. (1992). *I can't get over it: A handbook for trauma survivors.* Oakland, CA: New Harbinger Publications.

McCann, I. L. & Pearlman, L. A. (1990). *Psychological trauma and the adult survivor: Theory, therapy, and transformation.* New York: Brunner/Mazel, Publishers.

Parkinson, F. (1993). *Post-trauma stress: A personal guide to reduce the long-term effect and hidden emotional damage caused by violence and disaster.* Tucson, Arizona: Fisher Books.

Slover, C. & Tasci, D. (1999). *Trauma recovery handbook.* Denver, Colorado: Nicoletti-Flater Associates, Publishers.

Trauma Recovery (Child)
Monahan, C. (1993). *Children and trauma: A parent's guide to helping children heal.* New York: Lexington Books.

Terr, L. (1990) *Too scared to cry: Psychic trauma in childhood.* New York: Harper and Row, Publishers.

Debriefing

Mitchell, J. T. & Everly, G. (1995*). Critical incident stress debriefing: An operations manual for the prevention of traumatic stress among emergency services and disaster workers (2nd Ed).* Ellicott City, Maryland: Chevron Publishing Corporation.

ABOUT THE AUTHOR

Dr. Kelly A. Zinna earned her doctorate in clinical psychology from the University of Denver. Her background includes a specialty in violence prediction, including her tenure at a state hospital for the criminally insane. Dr. Zinna has received specialized training in criminal profiling and hostage negotiation from the FBI.

Dr. Zinna presently performs violence risk assessments for corporations and local, state and federal law enforcement agencies. She also specializes in the identification and prevention of Workplace and Schoolplace Violence. Dr. Zinna has conducted hundreds of training workshops for municipalities, public and private agencies, Fortune 500 companies, educational institutions and police academies. Dr. Zinna has frequently been called to testify as an expert witness in criminal and civil trials. Dr. Zinna is a member of the Association of Threat Assessment Professionals and the International Association of the Chiefs of Police.

Dr. Zinna is the founder of **Violence Prevention and Intervention, Inc.,** a psychological firm based in Denver, Colorado (**_www.campusviolence.com_**). **VPI** specializes in the prediction of violence potential. Services include training on Workplace and Schoolplace Violence issues, policies and procedures, and consultation on managing potentially violent employees and students.

To order additional copies of *After Columbine*, please visit our website at
www.campusviolence.com or fill out the order form below, enclose a check or
money order payable to Spectra Publishing Co., Inc., and mail to Spectra at P.O.
Box 966, Silverthorne, CO 80498.

ORDER FORM

AFTER COLUMBINE

Number of Copies _____ x $30.00/copy = _____

Sales Tax (Colorado Residents only) at 7.5 % = _____

Shipping and Handling = _____ $3.50

Total _____

Mail order form with check or money order to:

Spectra Publishing Co., Inc.
P.O. Box 966
Silverthorne, CO 80498

A portion of the proceeds of *After Columbine* will be donated by the author
and publisher to various Columbine related charities and violence prevention
agencies.

Please allow 3 weeks for delivery of order.